Races of Africa

C. G. SELIGMAN

Races of Africa

Fourth Edition

London
OXFORD UNIVERSITY PRESS
New York Toronto
1966

Oxford University Press, Ely House, London W.1

GLASGOW NEW YORK TORONTO MELBOURNE WELLINGTON
CAPE TOWN SALISBURY IBADAN NAIROBI LUSAKA ADDIS ABABA
BOMBAY CALCUTTA MADRAS KARACHI LAHORE DACCA
KUALA LUMPUR HONG KONG

First Published in the Home University Library *1930*
Second Edition 1939
Third Edition 1957
Fourth Edition in Oxford Paperbacks University Series *1966*

PRINTED IN GREAT BRITAIN BY NEILL & CO LTD EDINBURGH

960
se 465 m

Contents

1	Introduction	1
2	Bushmen, Hottentots, and Negrillos	11
3	The True Negro	30
4	The True Negro (*continued*)	49
5	Hamites (Eastern Hamites)	61
6	Hamites (Northern Hamites)	81
7	Nilo-Hamites and Nilotes	100
8	Bantu	117
9	Bantu (*continued*)	137
10	Semites	150

Appendix 1 Literature 160
Appendix 2 Height Conversion Table 163

Index 164

Maps:
1. Distribution of Languages 6
2. Geographical Factors 9
3. Nilo-Hamites, Nilotes, and Bantu 103

20739

Publisher's Note to the Third Edition

In this new revised edition of Professor Seligman's *Races of Africa*, the general arrangement and as much as possible of the original wording and content have been retained. Many changes were rendered inevitable by the marked advance since 1930 in our knowledge of African peoples, an advance due largely to the work of Professor Seligman's own students, and a new reading-list has also been provided; but the aim has been to produce the sort of revision that he himself might have attempted had he undertaken it. It is an index of his scholarship and expertise in all fields of anthropology that what he could do almost single-handed has now required the collaboration of many.

Professor Seligman, in the first edition, acknowledged the help and advice of Dr. C. K. Meek, Miss P. Puckle, Miss M. L. Tildesley, and the late Messrs. J. H. Driberg and E. Torday. Those who have contributed to the present revision include J. C. Trevor (physical anthropology); E. Gellner and J. Nicolaisen (North Africa); E. E. Evans-Pritchard (North and East Africa); P. Bohannan, D. Forde, M. Fortes, P. Kaberry, the late S. F. Nadel, and D. J. Stenning (West Africa); J. H. Beattie, G. W. B. Huntingford, L. P. Mair, and J. G. Peristiany (East Africa); J. A. Barnes, I. Cunnison, and M. Douglas (Central Africa); and I. Schapera (South Africa).

September 1956

1
Introduction

THE AUTHOR OF A VOLUME such as the present is from the very beginning confronted by certain difficulties which it is well that the reader should appreciate in order to make the necessary allowances and corrections. It is obvious that questions of race should first and last be determined by the study of physical characters, yet in no part of Africa is there in existence anything approaching an anthropological survey based on such characters, nor can it be said for any considerable area that even the first rough survey work has been done. If our ignorance is not quite so dense on the cultural side, even here there are unsurveyed areas and uncharted tribes; on the other hand, we do possess excellent monographs dealing with particular peoples, and with each of these as a nucleus for its own region it is sometimes possible to work out a reasonable scheme for certain areas. On the linguistic side things are rather better, but language—helpful as it may be— is itself no safe guide to race. Yet the study of the races of Africa has been so largely determined by the interest in speech, and it is so much easier to acquire a working knowledge of a language than of any other part of man's cultural make-up, that names based upon linguistic criteria are constantly applied to large groups of mankind and, indeed, if intelligently used, often fit quite well. Hence, in describing the great racial groups of Africa, terms such as 'Bantu', which strictly speaking have no more than a linguistic significance, are habitually employed, and in this volume linguistic criteria will play a considerable part in the somewhat mixed classification adopted.

The second obstacle consists in the presentation of the material, and the necessity to rely on words alone to bring definite physical types before the mind of the reader without the help which, in a larger and more costly volume, would be rendered by photographs and drawings. While this difficulty cannot be avoided it seems possible to lessen it by the careful definition in this introductory chapter of such terms as 'tall', 'short', 'round-headed', 'broad-nosed', etc. It will also be advisable to point out that a few words are used in a technical sense. Thus, 'clan' signifies a group recognizing descent in one line (whether patrilineal or matrilineal), within which intermarriage is not allowed, such groups being combined in one larger unit, usually the tribe. 'Totem' refers to an animal or plant species of which *all* (individual) members are considered of one blood with *all* the members of a human group (generally coinciding with a 'clan' as defined above). 'Fetish', so common a word in books on West Africa, is purposely avoided; at best it represents a particular aspect of animism, the belief in separable indwelling spirits in animate and inanimate objects, including some made by human hands. It will be well to add that religion, to which we shall so often refer, has in Africa no necessary connexion with morality as we understand the term; it is not in fact a moral code externally imposed and controlled, and for the most part embodying a revelation, but rather an explanation of the facts of existence and a commentary on life, controlling action, the beliefs and practices which it embodies being simply part of the texture of daily existence. There is usually nothing comparable to our ideas of the retributive justice of a God, punishing evil and rewarding good, and where any such idea appears it is important to exclude Christian and Muhammadan influence before accepting it as part of the African scheme of things. It is even probable that such undeveloped beliefs as that of the Kru, that the souls of the good ascend the heavens via the Milky Way, which is the path of ghosts, may be due to foreign influence.

Omitting blood groups and other serological data, which have yet to be synthesized for the greater part of Africa, the chief criteria of race considered in this book include skin colour, hair form, stature, head shape, and certain characters of the face, e.g. prognathism, and of the nose.

Skin Colour. This will be referred to by the terms in general use.

Hair Form. Three broad divisions are generally recognized: 'straight', 'wavy' or 'curly', and 'spiralled', of which only the last two are truly applicable to native African populations.

Stature. Here it is well to be precise. If measurements are available, the terms 'short', 'tall', etc., will be used to denote the customary anthropological categories for adult males in accordance with the following limits:

Pygmy	. .	under 150 cm.	(under 59 in.)
Short	. .	150 to 160 cm.	(59 to 63 in.)
Medium	.	160 to 170 cm.	(63 to 67 in.)
Tall	. . .	170 to 180 cm.	(67 to 71 in.)
Very Tall	.	180 cm. or over	(71 in. or over)

Heights are given throughout the text in inches rather than in units of the metric system, but a conversion table of those between 5 and 6 feet will be found in Appendix 2.

That there is a considerable range of stature among most peoples is obvious, but in this and other measurements averages based on fifty or more adults of the same sex, chosen at random, usually give reliable estimates of the population represented if it is homogeneous; moreover, a tall group will not as a rule contain very short persons (apart from dwarfs), nor a pygmy group tall ones.

Head Shape. Looked at from the side some heads will be seen to be long—the hair must be discounted—and others short, while seen from above such heads look long and (more or less) round respectively. The various degrees of this distinction in shape are expressed by the cephalic index (C.I.), which is the percentage ratio of the greatest breadth of the head or skull (B) to its greatest length (L), i.e. C.I. $= (100 \times B)/L$. Except in artificially deformed heads it is uncommon for this figure not to fall between 65 and 90, and most values range from 70 to 85. The terminology applied to different limits of the C.I. for skulls (strictly the cranial index) is:

Long or dolichocephalic . . under 75
Medium or mesocephalic . 75 to 80
Round or brachycephalic . 80 or over

The value of indices taken on living subjects is about two units higher; hence dolichocephalic and brachycephalic heads (as opposed to skulls) are, respectively, under 77, and 82 or over.

Face. Though a number of indices are used to indicate the proportions of the face, it does not seem necessary to employ them in this book, the terms 'broad-faced' and 'narrow-faced' being self-explanatory, while all must have noticed the varying projection of the forehead and the zygomatic or cheek bones. Projection of the face below the forehead, and especially of the jaws (prognathism), is common in Africa and may be allied with a bulging forehead.

Nose. The nose may be high or low, broad or narrow, with its bridge flat, medium, or projecting. The percentage ratio of breadth (NB) to height (NH) is the nasal index, i.e. $N.I. = (100 \times NB)/NH$. This is so important that it seems well to give the terms and figures commonly employed for its divisions. Since there is no simple relationship between measurements of the nose taken on the living (height from root to junction of the septum and lip, and breadth between the wings) and those taken on the skull, and values for the N.I. for the one cannot be easily converted into those for the other, only limits for the living are given:

Narrow-nosed or leptorrhine . . under 70
Medium-nosed or mesorrhine . 70 to 85
Broad-nosed or platyrrhine . . 85 or over

Noses that are broader than they are high (hyperplatyrrhine) are not very uncommon among Negroes. The nasal index has proved of special use in areas in which the population is of mixed origin, e.g. East Africa.

These, then, are the limited, and, at least outwardly, simple criteria that we shall use to study the races of Africa and their constituent peoples. For descriptive purposes it is scarcely possible to do more than slightly modify A. C. Haddon's definition and say that race connotes 'a group of peoples who have certain well-marked physical characters in common'.

Within such limitations the greatest divisions of mankind inhabiting Africa, its principal races from the standpoint of the distinctness of each from the others and their importance, are as follows:

(1) Hamites⎫
(2) Semites ⎭—these have a common origin.
(3) Negroes
(4) Bushmen ⎫
(4a) Hottentots⎭—sometimes known as Khoisan.
(5) Negrillos.

It must, however, be remembered that one race, the Semitic, apart from a certain amount of mixture in Ethiopia, has only been present in Africa for little over 1,000 years.

The distribution of the languages spoken by these great divisions is well shown in Professor Struck's map reproduced overleaf. A comparison of the linguistic areas defined on this map with the details given in each chapter will roughly indicate how important a part linguistics play in our classification, and it is on account of this importance that the following brief diagnosis of the character of the prime languages of Africa is given.

The Hamitic languages are inflected: nouns have grammatical sex-gender, which, with number and case, is expressed by suffixes; verbs are conjugated by both prefixes and suffixes and have a number of derivative forms, e.g. intensive, reflexive, causative, etc.

The Semitic languages so closely resemble the Hamitic (inflexion, grammatical sex-gender, etc.) that there can be no doubt that they are closely related (and may indeed be considered to have a not very remote common ancestor), but they differ in that the Semitic have 'triliteral roots', i.e. 'the root of a verb (which is found in the third person singular of the "perfect" tense) normally consists of three consonants, as in the Arabic *qatala* "he killed", *nasara* "he helped". . . . Verbs consisting of more than three consonants are either "derived forms" or of a later formation; those with only two radicals are probably contracted. These triliteral roots seem to be quite peculiar to the Semitic family.' (Werner)

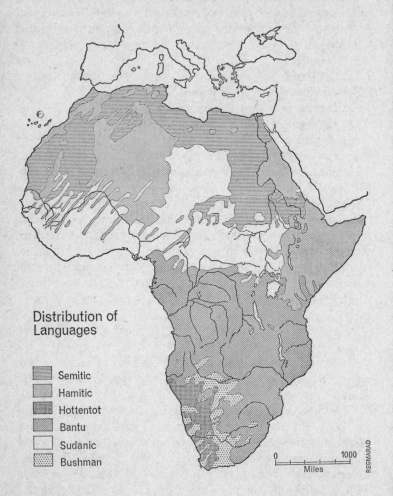

Distribution of
Languages

▨ Semitic
▨ Hamitic
▨ Hottentot
▨ Bantu
☐ Sudanic
▨ Bushman

0   1000
Miles

REGMARAD

Fig. 1

The Negro languages, i.e. those spoken by the true Negro, and also by many other blacks (e.g. the Nilotes), are generally termed Sudanic. Attempting to define these we may say that all words are built up on a monosyllabic basis, that there is an absence of inflexion—including grammatical gender—and that the genitive is placed before its governing noun. None of these three criteria must be taken too absolutely—languages of a perfectly pure type are rare—but, broadly speaking, the Sudanic languages all tend to exhibit the above three features, so that, ignoring exceptions and traces of borrowing which we find in individual languages, we may hold to the criteria given. Among the most typical Sudanic languages are those of the West African Twi and Yoruba. Here the greater number of words, and especially the verbs, are simple monosyllables, consisting of a consonant followed by a vowel, which, as Ellis points out, are like the syllables in a child's first reading book: *ba, be, bi, bo, bu*, etc. But since the number of such combinations is limited, the languages of these Africans have become tonic, i.e. the Negro has hit on the same expedient for modifying sounds and multiplying meanings as the Chinese: the pitch of the voice is used to change entirely the meaning of a word. Thus, *da* with a low tone means 'throw', with a high tone, 'cruel'; *do* with a low tone, 'to be sad', but with a level intonation, 'sleep'.

The Bushman languages cannot be adequately characterized in the present stage of our knowledge. They are largely mono-syllabic, lack prefixes and grammatical sex-gender, but make extensive use of suffixes, particles, and reduplication. Their 'clicks' (p. 12) are proper to themselves to the extent that they exist in no other languages except those of the Hottentots and the Sandawe and Hatsa of Tanzania, and some Bantu, to whom the Bushmen have communicated them.[1]

Hottentot, in the past, was sometimes regarded as a Hamitic language which had borrowed clicks and certain other elements from Bushman; but 'in view of the overwhelming vocabulary resemblance to Bushmen languages, the fundamental role of clicks in Hottentot phonology, and the detailed morphological

[1] The signs used before certain words in Chapter 2 and at the end of Chapter 4, e.g. ‖gauab, are conventional signs for particular clicks.

agreements with Bushmen, there can be no doubt that Hottentot is a member of the Khoisan family of languages.' (Greenberg)

Nothing is known of any language proper to the Negrillos.

Of the divisions of the races of Africa given on p. 5, Nos. 1, 3, and 4 are by far the most important; indeed it would not be very wide of the mark to say that the history of Africa south of the Sahara is no more than the story of the permeation through the ages, in different degrees and at various times, of the Negroes and the Bushmen by Hamitic blood and culture. The Hamites were, in fact, the great civilizing force of black Africa from a relatively early period, the influence of the Semites being late and in the main confined to the 'white' areas north of the Sahara inhabited by Hamitic peoples.

Turning to geographical factors, the sketch map (Fig. 2) on p. 9 shows in a very summary and diagrammatic manner some of the main features of Africa that are of importance as conditioning or explaining the distribution of its peoples. Here are no great mountain ranges to obstruct free communications, and the real difficulties of the continent—as explorers have always found—are its deserts and forests. In the north the Sahara in the main separates Negro-land from the Mediterranean populations. The highland steep-edged massif of Ethiopia, with a strip of rain forest (not shown in Fig. 2) on its western edge, has acted to a considerable extent as a barrier to the spread of Negro tribes into this part of Ethiopia. The Nile-Congo watershed, with its narrow zones of rain forest on the banks of the north-flowing tributaries of the Bahr-el-Ghazal, though only 1,500–2,000 feet high, has proved an efficient obstacle to the western extension of the Nilotes. The remains of the Bushman tribes still cling to the barren uplands of South-West Africa and the Kalahari Desert. The distribution of the domestic animals, and therefore the mode of life and the politico-economic system, can also be correlated with the type of country. Thus, only camel-nomads can exist in the Sahara, apart from oases, while cattle are not to be found in the tropical rain forest, but constitute the most important element in the life of the Bantu and Nilo-Hamites of the South and East African mountain savannahs and parklands.

In conformity with the point of view set forth above we

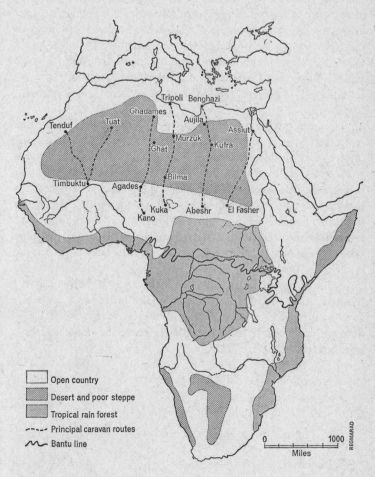

Open country

Desert and poor steppe

Tropical rain forest

----- Principal caravan routes

~~ Bantu line

0   1000
        Miles

REGMARAD

Fig. 2 *Geographical Factors*

should first describe Negrillos and Bushmen—the most techno-
logically retarded of Africans—then Negroes and Hamites, and
after them such peoples as the Hottentots, Bantu, etc., who have
arisen by mixture of these races. Actually the Hottentots so
closely resemble the Bushmen that in a small work such as this it
is inadvisable to separate them, and therefore the order followed
will be: Bushmen, Hottentots, and Negrillos; Negroes; Hamites;
hamiticized Negroes (Nilo-Hamites, Nilotes, and Bantu);
Semites.

No mention will be made of the fossil remains of African man
which have been discovered of late years, nor of the myriad stone
implements of palaeolithic age that have been found in various
parts of the continent. It will, however, be well to point out that
though the Bushman has persisted to the present day he belongs
to a type so ancient that he may well have been in Africa for a
period to be measured in tens of thousands of years; and until
less than a hundred years ago he was using stone tools of the same
type as were being made in Europe during the later period of the
Old Stone Age.

It will be obvious that this book is intended to be read with a
map, or rather with the African portion of the best atlas available.
It is for this reason, and to facilitate reference, that political and
geographical boundaries are cited even where they have no ethnic
significance.

2
Bushmen, Hottentots, and Negrillos

IT IS GENERALLY AGREED that the Bushmen reached their present habitat in South Africa from the north, their ancestors having perhaps occupied the greater part of tropical East, East-Central, and Northern Africa. In support of this view may be cited the discovery of 'Bushman' rock-paintings in Tanzania and Ethiopia and of perforated stone spheres—typical Bushman digging-stick weights—there and even in Uganda and southern Sudan. In spite of this there does not seem to be any valid reason for regarding the Bushmen as closely related to the Negrillos of the Central African forest, though as is but natural this view has been held fairly widely; on the other hand, there seems no doubt that the extinct Strandloopers of the south and western coasts of Cape Province were but a group of Bushmen who adopted a special mode of life, with consequent modifications of culture, suitable to the narrow coastal zone in which they settled.

The former extension of the people over practically the whole of South Africa is shown by the distribution of their relics, especially rock-paintings, skeletal remains, and even place-names. Apart from isolated offshoots and stray individuals their present range is restricted to southern Angola, the central and northern portions of the Kalahari Desert, and the northern half of South-West Africa, where according to Tobias as many as 50,000 are thought to survive. It is only here that their original mode of life has been retained, and even these groups have been affected racially and culturally by contact with the Bantu.

The Bushman is so distinctive in appearance as to be distinguished at a glance from all other Africans, save only the Hottentot. He is short, averaging about 62 inches (and therefore not pygmy), with slightly built well-shaped limbs and small hands and feet. The skin is yellow or yellowish-brown, and wrinkles particularly easily; the hair of the head is so tightly spiralled that it forms tufts or 'peppercorns', which appear to leave bare patches on the surface of the scalp. The head is mesocephalic (C.I. 75–76), low in the crown and pentagonal as seen from above; the face is orthognathous, small and broad, with prominent cheek-bones, very flat nose, low but bulging forehead, and pointed chin. The eyes are narrow and the lids display a variety of folds; the lobe may be absent from the small squarish ear. The usual forward curvature of the lower end of the spine is exaggerated, making the buttocks specially prominent, and with the women there is often that considerable accumulation of fat on the buttocks and thighs to which is given the name steatopygia. The normal 'set' of the penis is horizontal rather than diagonal or pendulous in adult males, and the scrotum is contracted. In the north greater stature, darker skin, and lower cephalic index, go with admixture of Bantu blood.

It must ever be a subject of regret that the social habits of these interesting people were not properly observed and recorded some three generations ago, before the aggression of White Man and Bantu had combined so to reduce their numbers and break down their organization that much of the highest scientific value has been lost for ever. For this reason an attempt has been made in the following pages to give a fairly full summary of what has been saved, it being held that the intrinsic interest and importance of the Bushman warrants an allocation of what might otherwise be regarded as an undue proportion of the limited space of this work.

Linguistically the Bushmen are divided into three main groups: Southern, Northern, and Central, each comprising a number of separate 'tribes'. Each tribe speaks its own language and has its own name. So little is agreed concerning the Bushman tongues that no short statement of their grammatical peculiarities is possible, but all have the celebrated 'clicks' (Arbousset, an early French missionary, speaks of them clucking like turkeys), really suction sounds whose nature will be best understood by saying that the lateral click is the sound that is sometimes used among ourselves to urge on a horse.

The Southern group, formerly occupying Cape Province, is almost extinct; the Northern group centres in the north-east of South-West Africa and includes the relatively well-known Heikum, Auen, and Kung, while the Central (Kalahari) group includes the Naron (Aikwe), Tannekwe, Hukwe, Galikwe, and Hiechware.

The social organization and material culture of the Bushmen are very simple. They live in small communities or hunting bands consisting as a rule of from 50 to 100 persons. A number of these bands, united by a common name and language, form a tribe, but the tribe has little importance in regulating social life, and the bands are completely independent and autonomous. Within a band the only division is into families, consisting each of a man, his wife or wives, and their dependent children. The life of the band is usually directed by the older and more experienced men, and although among some of the north-west tribes each band has a hereditary chief he lacks judicial authority and in effect is merely a leader in hunting, war, and certain forms of ritual.

The Bushmen do not practise agriculture or animal husbandry, but obtain their livelihood by hunting and by gathering edible roots and vegetables. This mode of life makes them necessarily a nomadic people, and each band claims the hunting rights over a particular stretch of territory of which they know and respect the exact limits. Their dwellings are crude semi-circular shelters of branches put up by the women, generally near a waterhole; each family has its own shelter. Their chief weapon is the bow and poisoned arrow, the poison being obtained from snakes, plants, and among the Kalahari tribes from the grub or chrysalis of a small green beetle. Throwing-sticks and spears are also employed as instruments of hunting, as are traps, snares, and pitfalls. Gathering vegetable food is mainly women's work, for which a pointed digging-stick, sometimes weighted with a perforated stone, is used. Fire is obtained by fire-sticks, The food is usually shared by all present, but a man has the right to the skin of any animal that he kills, and from this he makes the clothing for himself and his family.

Clothing is scanty. The men wear a three-cornered piece of skin drawn between the legs and tied round the waist, the women a small apron in front and a larger one behind; both sexes also have cloaks of skins sewn together. All women and children, and the younger men, wear ornaments, usually chains made of ostrich egg-shell beads. Some tribes adorn themselves with black and red paint, chiefly on the face, and tattooing (for ornament) is also practised, ash being rubbed into the wounds. Among the Naron the old men tattoo a successful hunter in return for an offering of game.

Initiation ceremonies for girls at puberty are common for all Bushmen, but corresponding ceremonies for boys appear to be restricted to the Northern tribes. Circumcision is not practised, though the Hiechware have adopted this custom from their Bantu neighbours. At puberty the special tribal marks are cut on the foreheads of the boys by the medicine man, and they are then kept secluded for a month or two, during which time they live a life of hardship in the bush and are instructed in the lore of the tribe. A period of seclusion in her hut and the observance of certain food taboos is also part of the ceremony for girls, and among the north-western tribes a religious dance, known as the 'eland bull' dance, in which the male performers tie elands' horns or imitations thereof to their heads, is performed in their honour. After initiation, boys and girls are considered marriageable.

Monogamy is the general rule, though polygamy is not forbidden. Marriage within the band is forbidden in the Northern tribes, so that a man must seek his bride from a neighbouring band. On marriage he must make her a present of a *kaross* (skin cloak), and among some tribes he must shoot a buck and present it to the bride's parents for a marriage feast. The young couple usually live with the bride's people for the first few months. Children belong to the father. Widows generally remarry, and the second husband is then responsible for her children; but if she does not remarry, her husband's brother is expected to help support them. Brothers and sisters must avoid each other's company when grown up, as must mother-in-law and son-in-law.

Birth generally takes place in the bush, the child being nursed by its mother until three or four years of age. Should a second child be born before the first is weaned it is usually killed, and large families are therefore rare, three children being the average number.

When a death occurs the corpse is buried near the hut in a sleeping position, lying on its side with the knees drawn up. All a man's possessions are buried with him. Stones are laid on the grave to keep animals away, and the band then moves to another locality, abandoning the spot for a couple of years.

Medicine men and women are found among all Bushmen. Their most important function is rain-making and the regulation of the initiation ceremony for boys; they are also the doctors of the community, their favourite curative method being to draw out the disease and cast it away. They do not live or dress differently from the rest of the band and at the present day do not seem to have much influence.

Our knowledge of religious beliefs and customs of the Bushmen is very limited. They all pray to the moon and to other celestial bodies, and have a series of myths and legends relating to them. They also believe in certain mythical beings—known variously to different tribes as Cagn (the mantis), Gaunab, Huwu, Hishe, Tora, etc.—who appear to be personifications of natural forces, especially those producing rain, and are frequently invoked. Some of these beings are credited with creative powers and are met with in various myths of origin. Food taboos and certain hunting observances are recorded from some of the Northern tribes, and among all Bushmen there is a well-developed ritual relating to animals and other sources of food.

They are a cheerful, merry people, with a passionate love of dancing, which among all tribes is common both as a social amusement and in connexion with religious rites. Many of these dances take the form of masquerade, for the Bushmen possess extraordinary powers of mimicry, and are able to reproduce with accuracy the appearance, manners, and cries of the animals or persons they wish to represent. At one time the wearing of a skin was a common ruse to permit approach to game; a well-known rock-painting in the Herschel district of Cape Province shows a Bushman wearing an ostrich skin while stalking a flock of these birds. They all sing, though their tunes are not easy for Europeans to distinguish, and they have various musical instruments, the most prevalent being variants of the musical bow.

The culture of the Southern Bushmen is notable for the paintings and engravings which in the past they executed on the walls of caves and rock shelters. The paintings are naturalistic, often polychrome studies of high artistic merit, and many are of comparatively recent date. Among the subjects depicted are cattle-raids, dances, and magico-religious scenes in which animal-headed human figures are represented; but for the most part the artists recorded the animals which they hunted and upon which they subsisted. Although the practice of the art seems to have died out completely (among the Northern tribes apparently it never existed) there is ample evidence to prove that these widely distributed rock-paintings were the work of Bushmen. At the present day almost the only form of decorative art found consists of incised patterns on the ostrich egg-shells used for storing water.

The physical characters of the Hottentots are for the most part the same as those of the Bushmen, the chief points of difference being a taller stature (about 64 inches), a longer and narrower head (C.I. 73), and a rather more prognathous face. The Sandawe, recently studied by Trevor, are taller still (65 inches), and have a cephalic index of 75, similar to that of the Bushmen but higher than that of the Hottentots, whom they otherwise resemble. Apart from Bantu admixture in certain groups there is little doubt that the Hottentots are the result of the mixture of Bushmen with early invading Hamites, from whom they received those linguistic and cultural features that distinguish them from Bushmen. It is generally held that the mixed race arose in the north, perhaps in the neighbourhood of the Great Lakes, and that the Hottentots did not reach South Africa until after the Bushmen, crossing the upper waters of the Zambezi and reaching the west coast, then pressing forward to the south where they were found by the first Europeans to visit the Cape.

The former distribution of the Hottentots comprises practically the whole of the western part of South Africa from the

Kunene River in the north to the Cape Peninsula in the south, and extends inland to the Kei River. At the present time, while scattered remnants are found over a considerable part of this territory, the tribal organization is met with in any state of preservation only in South-West Africa north of the Orange River. Although many tribes existed, all spoke one of four closely related languages, and it is from these latter that the customary division of the Hottentots into four main groups—Naman, Korana, Gonaqua, and Old Cape Hottentots—is derived. The survivors in South-West Africa belong to the Naman group, and according to the most recent estimates number about 24,000. The old Hottentot population of the Cape has become largely absorbed by racial admixture with incoming Europeans and East Indian slaves, and has thus constituted the basis of the present 'Cape Coloured', 'Griqua', and 'Rehoboth' half-breeds.

The Hottentots are a passing people, and only a remnant of their former customs and beliefs survives. The only group whose social organization is at all well known is the Naman, of whom careful study was made by Mrs. Hoernlé, from whose account the following sketch is largely drawn.

The Naman consist of several groups or 'tribes', each with its own name and chief but bearing the common name of Nama and traditionally descended from one line of ancestors. Each tribe claims certain large fountains or pools as its property, and used to wander from fountain to fountain seeking pasture for its stock. The tribe is composed of a number of patrilineal and exogamous clans, one of which claims seniority, the chieftainship of the whole tribe being hereditary in this clan. The head of the senior clan is accorded a good deal of respect, but he cannot do much without the co-operation of the heads of the other clans, and the conduct of affairs in the tribe is in the hands of the old men generally. The tribe is not a centralized unit, and though occasionally the whole tribe camps together and at such times the clans camp in definite order round the huts of the chief's clan, as a rule the families composing a clan tend to live together in a separate part of the tribal territory. Each family has its own hut, where the children remain until they are married, though sometimes marriageable girls will share a hut together.

The kinship system is classificatory in principle. One term is applied to all grandparents and one to all grandchildren, sex being distinguished by grammatical suffixes; ortho-cousins are called by the same terms as brother and sister, but cross-cousins are distinguished, and marriage was formerly permitted with the cross-cousin. There is a special term for mother's brother and another for father's sister. The relative ages of the person speaking and the person addressed are carefully recognized in the terminology.

Culturally, the outstanding difference between Bushmen and Hottentots is that the former are hunters and food collectors only, while the latter are a pastoral people, with herds of long-horned cattle and flocks of fat-tailed sheep. They also differ from the Bushmen in practising the art of smelting iron for the manufacture of implements, blades of spears, and arrow-heads; they make pots and other vessels from wood, sometimes with incised designs, weave mats and baskets from reeds and rushes, and from skins make bags as receptacles for milk and water. On the whole, therefore, their material culture is superior to that of the Bushmen. They do not, however, appear ever to have possessed the art of painting or engraving on rock, in which the Bushmen excelled.

The principal food of the Hottentots is milk, which they keep in wooden pots and dishes and drink after allowing it to thicken. In contrast to most Bantu tribes of South Africa the milking is done by the women, not the men. They supplement their milk diet by vegetable foods—roots and berries and the !naras melon —and by hunting and trapping animals; their methods of hunting are similar to those of the Bushmen, though their snares are more elaborate and they no longer use the bow and arrow. They do not kill their cattle for food except on the occasion of a feast, though animals that die through natural causes are eaten. In recent years their flocks have diminished, and they have taken in a small way to agriculture. They are to some extent nomadic owing to the necessity of fresh pasturage for their flocks and herds, but they do not wander about so freely as the Bushmen and their encampments are of a more permanent nature.

The encampment is enclosed in a circular fence of thorn in

which are two gateways, one to the north, the other to the south, the huts of the people being ranged clan by clan round the inner side of the fence and the cattle herded in the centre, with special enclosures provided for the calves and lambs. The huts, of bee-hive shape, are much superior to those of the Bushmen and are constructed of supple pieces of undressed wood planted in the ground, the tops bent inward and tied by thongs to short pieces laid horizontally, so that the frame forms a rough hemisphere, withies are twisted round the structure, over which are laid layers of rush mats. The floor is smeared with a mixture of cowdung and blood. The inmates sleep on mats round the centre hearth. On shifting camp the structure is taken to pieces and transported on oxen to the site of the next encampment.

Clothing (now generally European) formerly consisted entirely of skins, prepared by softening and scraping. The men wore a loin-cloth of hide, with perhaps a small cloak, the women a well-ornamented skin apron with larger cloaks hanging down before and behind. Skin caps and sandals are occasionally worn. Both sexes adorn their heads with copper trinkets and paint their bodies with ochre and fat; women wear ornaments of shells, etc., and strips of raw hide sewn round their legs, and men armlets of copper and ivory. No form of bodily mutilation appears now to be practised, although early writers speak of the excision of one testicle and the amputation of the joint of the little finger.

Marriages are arranged by the parents of the two parties concerned, the girl's people being required by custom to make a show of reluctance, ending, after persuasion by the boy's people, in acquiescence. During the period of betrothal the boy and girl may not communicate with one another except through an intermediary. The marriage is celebrated by a feast, provided by the bridegroom's parents—although the bride's parents sometimes contribute—and on the day of the wedding the husband and wife each present the other's mother with a cow, in token of the fact that she has nourished their spouse as a child. Marriage is usually patrilocal, and the reception of the bride into her husband's group is the occasion of a feast, in which only the married women take part, symbolizing the reception of the girl into the community of wives.

A man must treat his mother-in-law with the greatest deference; they are said to be shy of each other, and he must never look at her when addressing her.

The wife is the mistress of her hut and all its domestic utensils. She does the milking, and when the husband wishes to have milk he must ask her for it. In general it appears that women have a good deal of independence and are far from being dominated by their husbands.

The levirate is practised, i.e. a widow is inherited by a brother of her deceased husband.

A pregnant woman is subject to a number of taboos; for example she may not be present when any animal is being slaughtered, as this is supposed to affect her child adversely. Suckling is prolonged, but, in contrast with the Bushmen, it does not appear that infanticide is practised if a second child be born before the first has been weaned. Boys are named after their mother, girls after their father, so that all children of the same sex bear the same name, age distinctions being indicated by the use of additional qualifying words. Each child is allotted a special cow by his parents, and the milk from this cow is reserved for him.

Although formerly the aged were abandoned to perish of hunger, in family life respect for age is inculcated, and deference and respect must always be paid to elders. Thus the eldest brother has the honoured place and the first voice in any debate. There is, however, a strong taboo between brother and sister when once grown up, and they must avoid each other completely; a brother must never speak to his sister directly, be alone with her in the hut, or speak of her except in the most respectful terms:

The highest oath a man could take, and still takes, was to swear by his eldest sister. A man can never address his own sister personally; he must speak to another person to address the sister in his name, or in the absence of anybody he says, so that his sister can hear, 'I wish that somebody will tell my sister that I wish to have a drink or milk', etc. The eldest sister can even inflict punishment on a grown-up brother if he omits the established traditionary rules of courtesy and the code of etiquette.

This relation between a woman and her brother also affects the relations of children with their father's sister or mother's brother respectively. The father's sister is treated with much deference and respect, but on the other hand the greatest liberties are allowed with the mother's brother: a boy can do almost anything at his maternal uncle's home without being blamed for it, and can take without asking any specially fine animals from among his uncle's herds.

The ceremonies attached to such transitional phases as birth, puberty, marriage, remarriage, disease, etc., afford admirable examples of those rites called by Van Gennep *rites de passage*. In normal Hottentot society every person belongs as it were to a definite stratum, the members of which have definite duties, know exactly their place and the correct manner of behaving both towards their mates in their stratum and to those either below or above it. A person in a 'state of transition' from one stratum of society to another is said to be *!nau*, i.e. in a condition of taboo, dangerous both to himself and to all with whom he comes in contact. Thus, when a child attains the age of puberty he is no longer a child but neither is he a full member of the tribe, and so for a period he belongs nowhere but is removed from the solidarity and security of his former position and exposed to great peril. He is accordingly made to pass through certain ceremonies, the object of which is to initiate him with the least possible delay into the group of persons who are already in the same state as that which he has now entered. The essential aspects of these ceremonies are summed up as follows by Mrs. Hoernlé:

In childbirth, marriage, puberty, or bereavement rites, the new status has simply to be recognized, acknowledged, and the necessary steps taken to protect the individual and the society by receiving the man or woman into the new group to which he or she belongs. This is done by the preparation of a sacramental meal in which only persons duly qualified are allowed to share. In the other group of crises, a stage preliminary to the sacramental meal is necessary. The !nau person has first to be identified with the new group by injecting some of the 'essence' of that group into him. This is done by making incisions in some part of his body, the part varying with the crisis, and injecting a concoction of which one ingredient is invariably some of the grease and dirt scraped from the body of the officiating person. This is the practice in remarriage, in the puberty ceremonies of boys, in the reception into the rank of hunters, in the treatment of diseases which are regarded as

!nau, etc. .... The next stage in both groups is the renunciation of all that represents the old life, after a period more or less prolonged of complete seclusion. The individual must be reborn. There is a special cleansing of the !nau person's body by the individual officiating, after which a totally new set of clothing is put on. .... At the same time a house is thoroughly purified and what might be called an 'expiatory' meal is eaten. For this meal but one animal is killed, and of it none but the !nau person and persons who can no longer become !nau may partake. Finally there is the careful reintroduction of the person to all the familiar daily tasks which have been so long laid aside, and so life begins again with all the solidarity of the new group behind its new member.[1]

The transition rites, though varying in detail, have one feature in common, that the person must on no account touch water. Owing to the arid nature of their country and the uncertainty of the supplies on which their flocks and herds depend, water is endowed with a peculiar potency and sanctity by the Hottentots, and while in the normal routine it is used with little regard to ceremony it acquires on critical occasions a twofold significance, becoming on the one hand a source of protection to the tribe, and on the other hand a danger to those who are for one reason or another in a critical condition. Thus, cold water is a source of great danger to a *!nau* person; he must on no account come in contact with it, and after purification he must be reintroduced to it with much ceremony, being splashed all over by some qualified person. As an example of its powers may be cited the Hottentot witch-doctor, who, it is said, never washes or touches cold water. His potency resides as it were in the dirt and grease of his body, and this is always an ingredient in his medicine. Should he touch water his power would be diminished, and a Berseba witch-doctor found guilty of malpractice was ducked in the pond by the chief's orders, thereby completely losing his magical powers. His medicine can also be rendered innocuous by immersion in cold water. Similarly, to splash oneself with water gives protection from ghosts, and cold water is poured on a grave 'to cool the soul of the deceased' and prevent him from becoming troublesome. When a whirlwind comes sweeping through a kraal and passes by

[1] W. Hoernlé, 'Certain Rites of Transition and the Conception of !Nau among the Hottentots', *Harvard African Studies, Varia Africana, II* (1918).

a hut the inmates rush inside, get cold water, and throw it in the path of the wind; did they not do this someone would surely die. Another indication of the vast importance attached to rain by the Naman is found in the annual rain ceremony, the most important social event of the year, when the whole tribe assembles, and ewes in lamb which would on no account be killed at any other time are sacrificed in the interests of fertility and abundance.

The transition rites are well illustrated in the puberty ceremonies for girls. Ceremonies for boys seem to have lapsed since big-game hunting became impossible, but a girl when she first shows signs of puberty undergoes an elaborate ritual. She is at once cut off from the ordinary life of the kraal, is confined in a small dark hut built inside her mother's, must lie there quite still wrapped closely in her sheepskin blanket, and must not speak above a whisper. She is, however, visited by her friends, who grind sweet-smelling leaves and bark into powder for her, and with this powder she is copiously covered. All the time she is in the hut she must not touch cold water and must be protected in many other ways. When she is ready to come out, a matron who has been a successful married women and reared many children, but who is now past the age of child-bearing, and who has taken charge of the girl all through her seclusion, scours her body thoroughly with melted butter and wet cow-dung to cleanse her of her 'child dirt'. The girl is then given a complete set of new clothing and led into the outer hut by the matron, with whom she prepares a meal for the other women assembled to receive her. The matron must hold her hand and aid her with each thing she does. So she is made free to cook and prepare a meal once more. Similarly she is reintroduced to all her daily tasks by the old woman. They gather wood together, collect roots and berries together, and the old woman supports the girl's arm while she milks—this milk is *!nau*, and can only be drunk by the old woman and others of her age. In the evening when the time comes to fetch the evening supply of water the girl goes accompanied by the old women, the matron walking just in front of her and another old woman just behind, in single file. Arrived at the water the woman takes a branch and splashes the water over the girl, whose legs she also rubs with wet mud. Finally both of them take a branch and strike the water. She then fills the girl's bucket and her own, places one on the girl's head, and they return home. This reintroduction of the girl to cold water marks the end of her state of taboo (*!nau*). Hahn states that in some tribes girls who have reached puberty must run about naked in the first thunderstorm, so that their bodies are washed by the rain, the belief being that this will cause them to be fruitful and to have many children; he says that he has himself witnessed this running in the thunder rain, when the roaring of the thunder was defeaning and the whole sky seemed to be one continual sheet of lightning.

There do not appear to be any *!nau* ceremonies for persons marrying for the first time, but similar rites and precautions are observed when a man or woman remarries, and after a death not only the near relatives but also the larger family circle are affected and have to undergo ceremonial purification. When a child has died, both parents become *!nau* and have to be dealt with similarly.

At death the corpse is wrapped in skins, which are sewn together. The relatives and friends spend the night together outside the hut in which the corpse is laid, and carry on a ceremonial wailing, the body usually being buried the following afternoon. The grave is dug with a niche on one side, in which the corpse is nowadays placed on its back with the head towards the west; formerly it was always buried in a sitting position facing east. The niche is closed with bushes and a slab of stone, and a mound raised over the grave; on this everyone present places a stone or twig. Formerly the hut of the deceased person was deserted, and the camp moved, but nowadays the hut is moved to another part of the camp, and even this is not always done. On returning from the grave the relatives wash their hands in water in front of the dead man's hut, and wail and writhe in lamentation (nowadays they sing hymns). The man's relatives then slaughter animals according to their means, all the different families providing pots in which the blood, meat, and entrails are collected separately. The blood is heated to boiling-point, mixed with a certain herb, and stirred till the steam rises, when the relatives gather round the pots and cover their heads with their skins until they perspire. An old man, not a relative, takes potblack and makes a line on the stomach of each person. The relatives eat only the flesh, the other members of the kraal the entrails, while only the old man officiating and others of like age use the blood. These rites take place in the dead man's hut and the widow takes no part. A widow or widower is !nau for some time after death, during which time uncooked meat or cold water must not be touched, neither must they go among the cattle nor handle pots. The period of mourning is brought to a close by a thorough cleansing, followed by a meal and a ceremonial introduction to water and the duties of daily life, as in a girl's puberty ceremony, though with variations in detail.

In Hottentot mythology and religious practices there are found what can best be described as hero-gods, apparently derived partly from animistic beliefs and partly from the personification of natural forces producing rain. Of these the most frequently met with are Tsui-‖goab, Heitsi Eibib, and ‖gauab or gaunab. The last of these (also met with among the Bushmen) is nowadays (probably owing to missionary influence) regarded as 'the devil', but originally denoted the spirit of a dead person, sometimes also taking the form of the ill-omened whirlwind, and Mrs. Hoernlé has recently shown that there is a strong connexion between ‖gaunab and the ‖hei ‖nun, 'the ghosts which hover over the graves or come from them', much dreaded by the Naman. In their mythology ‖gaunab is regarded as a malevolent being, always in conflict with Tsui ‖goab—the great tribal hero to whom they pray for rain and food—who destroys him, but he comes to life again; and one form of the legend implies that the fight is an annual one. Heitsi Eibib is a mythical hero, believed to have lived on earth and to have died and risen again many times, and tales of his wonderful deeds were widely narrated. All the actions ascribed to him were those of a man, but of one endowed with supernatural power. His 'graves', large mounds of stone, are found all over the country, and no Hottentot will pass one without adding to it a stone or a branch, sometimes also muttering a prayer for good luck in hunting.

Moon worship seems to have been prevalent among the Hottentots at one time, as it is among the Bushmen, but the cult has apparently died out, though the moon figures prominently in one of their myths, where it is associated with the origin of death.

As might be expected, the pygmy Negrillos of Africa present a number of features of the highest interest. Hunters, trappers, and collectors, they are nowadays confined to the thickest tropical forests within 5° north and south of the Equator, but the folklore of Africa and classical tradition alike point to their much wider distribution a few thousand years ago. The story of the annual invasion of the country of the pygmies by cranes on their winter flight is at least as old as Homer, and such combats are not uncommonly represented on classical works of art, while long before this, in the Pyramid Age (i.e. in the third millennium B.C.), the Pharaohs were sending south—but certainly not so far south as the Congo Valley—for pygmies to dance before them. Harkhuf, a noble of Assiut and one of its most experienced caravan leaders, made four journeys to Yam, i.e. at least as far south as Upper Nubia, when besides 'every good thing' he brought back a 'dancing dwarf . . . from the land of Spirits'. The news preceded his return, so that the Pharaoh wrote to him to come immediately bringing the pygmy with him, directing him to take the most minute precautions for his safety:

Come northward to the court immediately; . . . thou shalt bring this dwarf with thee, . . . from the land of spirits, . . . to rejoice and gladden the heart of the king of Upper and Lower Egypt, Neferkere, who lives forever. When he goes down with thee into the vessel appoint excellent people, who shall be beside him on each side of the vessel; take care lest he fall into the water. When [he] sleeps at night appoint excellent people, who shall sleep beside him in his tent. . . . My majesty desires to see this dwarf more than the gifts of Sinai and of Punt. If thou arrivest at court this dwarf being with thee alive, prosperous and healthy, my majesty will do for thee . . . according to the heart's desire of my majesty to see this dwarf.

More modern accounts of the pygmies indicate why they were such favourites; Junker writes of their amazing talent for mimicry:

A striking proof of this was afforded by an Achua whom I had seen and measured four years previously in Rumbek, and now again met at Gamari's. His comic ways and quick movements made this little fellow the clown of our society. He imitated with marvellous fidelity the peculiarities of persons whom he had once seen; for instance the

gestures and facial expressions of Jussuf Pasha . . . and of Haj Halil at
their devotions, as well as the address and movements of Emin Pasha
'with the four eyes' (spectacles) . . . and now he took me off to the life,
rehearsing after four years, down to the minutest details, and with surprising accuracy, my anthropometric performance when measuring
his body at Rumbek.

Physically the Negrillos are truly pygmy, the average for males
being about 56½ inches. They have exaggerated limb proportions,
with arms which are very long in relation to the legs. Their skin
may be reddish, or yellowish-brown, or very dark, the body often
covered with a light downy hair. The head is usually mesocephalic (average C.I. 79); nose very broad with little or no
bridge, eyes rather large and prominent; face short, tending to be
broad and generally prognathous, often to such a degree that Sir
Harry Johnston proposed the term 'pygmy-prognathous' for a
group comprising these little people and certain low-type forest
Negroes. Steatopygia is said to occur, though it is not pronounced.

They live in small communities; Junker speaks of coming
'suddenly on about fifty little Akka huts which stood close
together in the forest'.

They hunt with bows and poisoned arrows, and, though
regarded as cunning and revengeful, generally live on good terms
with the surrounding Bantu tribes—to some degree their overlords and protectors—whose languages they speak and with
whom they exchange game for bananas, maize, etc.

On the sociological side our knowledge of the pygmies has
recently been increased by the observations of Father Paul
Schebesta, who has travelled much in the pygmy country for the
express purpose of getting to know something of the habits and
customs of these little people. In spite of their excitable tempera-
ment and sudden gusts of rage he found them always friendly.

Totemism seems widely spread, perhaps universal, and the
relation of the individual pygmy to his clan animal is typical of
the belief:

Sometimes one gets the impression that pygmy clans actually believe
that their totems were their ancestors. And most pygmies believe that
after death they will be metamorphosed either wholly or partially into

their totem animals. . . . In all the five camps in which I stayed I could
trace the same basic principles of totemism. . . . The Abfoka clan's
totem was the 'Butiu' bird, the Aforaka's totem was the chimpanzee,
while the Mantu clan had two totems—the 'Solio', an aquatic animal,
and the 'Sasu' plant. . . . The favourite totems are the leopard and the
chimpanzee.

All the members of a clan must show the deepest reverence for their
totem. On no account must it be killed or injured in any way, and, of
course, it must not be eaten. A pygmy dare not even eat or drink from a
vessel that has been touched by his totem.[1]

In spite of these typical forms of behaviour, clan exogamy is not
obligatory, though marriage within the family group is avoided as
constituting incest. Circumcision, which is widespread, seems
to have been adopted from the neighbouring Bantu.

Any discussion of the religion of the Negrillos is rendered
difficult, owing to the known presence of Bantu and even Hamitic
influence. If we attempt to eliminate all possible outside elements
not very much is left. Yet, since no people adopts from foreign
religion forms incongruous with its own mental make-up, we may
provisionally regard the following ideas and practices, described
in Father Schebesta's publications, as constituting the religion of
the pygmies, even if in part introduced.

There seems to be little of the ancestral cult so common among
the Bantu; rather do the pygmies stress the existence of a power
associated with the firmament—sometimes regarded as a creator-
god and sometimes as having the appearance of an old man with
a long beard—the Lord of the hurricane, lightning, and rainbow.
Sometimes he is given a name, at others termed 'Grandfather'.
To him offerings are made; for instance, part of the heart of a
slain animal or portions of honeycomb. Among the Efé group,
invocations are addressed to this being, known to them by the
name of Tore, who made all things and to whom everything
ultimately belongs. Thus, before hunting, 'Tore, give me food,'
while it is Tore who takes the dead to himself and who kills evil-
doers with his lightning. There is also a cult of the moon.

At the present day, pygmies bury in a grave with a side recess,
thus copying the local Bantu, but it seems that of old the body

[1] Paul Schebesta, *Revisiting my Pygmy Hosts*, p. 141 (1939).

was left in the hut of a near relative and the group moved to another site.

Concerning the vexed question whether there is a pygmy language or whether the pygmies all speak the Bantu of their Negro overlords, Father Schebesta regards Efé as the aboriginal pygmy tongue of the Ituri forest-dwellers, though admitting that an enormous amount of borrowing, especially of vocabulary, has taken place.

With regard to the position of the Negrillos in the natural history of man, while some authorities suppose them to have arisen from their taller Negro neighbours (by what can only be called degeneration), this view is not generally accepted, and in fact seems untenable.

3
The True Negro

THOUGH THE NEGRO is one of the most widespread stocks in Africa, no Negro skulls of any considerable age have yet been discovered; indeed an accepted authority has written of the earliest appearance of Negroes in history as taking place during the great period of Egyptian expansion, about 1500 B.C. This, however, is scarcely accurate, or becomes so only if special definitions be framed for 'history' and 'Negro', for on one of the great proto-dynastic slate palettes dating from *circa* 3200 B.C. are represented captives and dead with spiralled hair and showing the same form of circumcision as is now practised by the Masai and other Negroid tribes of Kenya and Tanzania. Thus, though there is not, and cannot be, any record of skin colour, there is every reason to believe that these men were as much 'Negroes' as many of the East African tribes of the present day to whom this name is commonly applied. Moreover, the first Archaeological Survey of Nubia brought to light a burial—with typical Negro hair—dating to the Middle Kingdom (about 2000 B.C.), while four Negro women were found in a single cemetery dated as far back as the late pre-dynastic period—say about 3000 B.C.

Racially Africa may be divided into two portions by a line drawn from the mouth of the Senegal River through Timbuktu to Khartoum, thence southwards and westwards to the Ethiopian border at about 12° N., from here following the western and then the southern border of Ethiopia to the Juba River and from the Juba River to the Indian Ocean. The northern division is essentially white or light-skinned, inhabited by Hamites and

Semites of 'European' type; the southern essentially Negro, with peoples almost everywhere characterized by their dark skin and spiralled hair. But though this line marks out the northern boundary of the Negro with a fair measure of precision it must be realized that the term 'Negro' includes at least three huge groups, each with its peculiar characteristics. Almost everywhere in this vast area the Negro carries in his veins a greater or lesser proportion of Hamitic blood and has been influenced by Hamitic culture. The true Negro is mainly confined to the neighbourhood of the Guinea coast, including Nigeria and the Western Sudan, with some part of the Cameroons and perhaps the Congo. The rest of Negro Africa consists of Negroes hamiticized to a varying extent: on the one hand the Bantu, on the other the Nilotes and 'Nilo-Hamites'.

West Africa, the home of the true Negro, may be regarded as extending from the mouth of the Senegal River, about 16° N., to the eastern boundary of Nigeria. So defined, its eastern boundary coincides with the northernmost limits of the Bantu along the lower course of the Rio del Rey. Politically, no part of Africa has been more confused, consisting as it does of a series of countries stretching back from the coast, each originating in coastal trading centres established between the fifteenth and eighteenth centuries and having belonged until their independent statehood to France or to Great Britain, together with a single remaining Portuguese possession and the Liberian Republic originally founded by liberated slaves. It is necessary to emphasize these facts since they explain the origin of such terms as 'Slave Coast' and 'Gold Coast', and render intelligible the arbitrary division of the area into states, irrespective of local ties or tribal association. These countries—from north to south and then westwards —are Senegal, Gambia, Portuguese Guinea, Guinea, Sierra Leone, Liberia, the Ivory Coast, Ghana, Togo, Dahomey, and Nigeria, all extending inland and embedded as it were in that great portion of Africa sometimes called the West Sudan.

In our present state of knowledge the first classification of the tribes indigenous to this vast area must be linguistic. From Senegal through the Guinea Coast and southern Nigeria, and occupying the hinterland from west to east, are found four major and two or three lesser language groups, all belonging to the Sudanic family and each comprising a number of related languages. An example is furnished by the Kwa group of the Guinea Coast, which includes the Twi-, Ewe-, and Yoruba-speaking peoples, who succeed each other from west to east. Each of these groups consists of a number of tribes speaking related dialects and with more or less similar customs, and the members of all three groups exhibit a substantial identity in their basic beliefs and habits of life, as well as in linguistic fundamentals. This cluster may indeed be regarded as the core of 'true Negro' peoples.

According to Haddon, the main physical characters of the true Negro are a black skin, spiralled hair, a tall structure averaging about 68 inches, moderate dolichocephaly (average cephalic index 74–75), a flat broad nose, thick and often everted lips, and frequently a considerable degree of prognathism. Culturally Negro peoples possess some characteristic features. They build gable-roofed huts; their traditional weapons include bows tapering at each end, with bowstrings of vegetable products, swords, and plaited shields, but no clubs or slings; among musical instruments are wooden drums and a peculiar form of guitar—the so-called West African harp—in which each string has its own support; clothing is of bark-cloth and palm-fibre, not of skin. Secret societies, masks, and wood-carvings of the human figure are characteristic, while coiled basketry and head-rests do not occur. Cattle and horses are rare, mainly because of endemic trypanosomiasis, the domestic animals being the dog, goat, pig, and hen; the plants originally cultivated were beans, gourds, bananas, and perhaps earth-nuts, though yams, manioc, cassava, and maize are also now well established. Cannibalism is said to have occurred in some areas. Human sacrifice, which was common, might attain a huge scale as in Ashanti. Circumcision and the knocking out of the upper incisors occur, though not very commonly.

On the artistic side the true (West African) Negro shows a skill in plastic art that is rarely found elsewhere in Negro Africa, the carved ivories, masks, and bronzes of Ife and Benin being especially noteworthy. In Benin, on the capture of the city in 1897, were found many carved elephant tusks, and bronzes cast by the *cire-perdue* process, including some, such as the well-known bronze head of a young Negro woman in the British Museum, showing high artistic feeling and great technical skill. The finest of these are to be assigned to the sixteenth century and, though undoubtedly Negro in execution, may show European, i.e. Portuguese, influence. Indeed, many of the bronze plaques portray Europeans or Negroes with guns, while some of the ivories can only represent objects of European manufacture. But the magnificent bronze heads found in Ife, the religious capital of the Yoruba, perhaps antedate these bronzes and testify to an indigenous tradition, possibly of North African derivation.

Secret societies are characteristic of many West African tribes and some description must be attempted. It is first necessary to realize that the term 'secret society' is used to denote a large variety of associations which often have no common function. Even the element of secrecy varies enormously, i.e. from a society to which all males should belong on payment of the usual fees, to an association with an elaborate ritual of initiation, possibly a private language, and a particular ceremonial and symbolism, the whole sometimes directed to purposes that were not only illegal from the white man's standpoint but are anti-social from the point of view of the Negro. It must, however, be admitted that the latter form of secret society is in the minority, and it must be remembered that the majority of secret societies are mutual benefit clubs, membership not only conferring social distinction but being regarded as a reasonable method of employing the wealth of a rich man and of benefiting the poor. Among the Yoruba the most important are the Ogboni and the Oro, while in Dahomey the cult of Yewe approximates to a secret society. Among the Ibibio in the east the Egbo is the most influential, with grades varying from six to eleven in number; it has judicial functions, and those who resist its findings are executed. In the west the so-called 'Poro Bush' of Mende, Bulom, and Temne involves the initiation of all youths and maidens into tribal obligations and in secret, in the lower ranks only, in the same sense as initiation schools all over Africa. In the higher ranks, to which only some people aspire, these societies have judicial and often religious and medicinal roles. Human Leopard societies, which have in the past caused considerable trouble to West African administrators, seem to be only a particular example—in the least desirable form —of a West African secret society. Masks are often associated with secret societies, and, as already mentioned, secret societies and masks are two of the cultural features distinguishing West Africa and the Congo from East Africa. It is noteworthy that the titles of some of these societies are derived from occupational guilds, one of the highest titles being that of 'blacksmith'. In spite of all that has in the past been said against secret societies it must not be forgotten that in the majority of instances they are probably more beneficial than harmful. For example, the much abused Poro society, as part of its task of helping to maintain law and order, will taboo fishing when there is danger of the waters being fished out, and by the exhibition of the society's signs will prevent the destruction of a crop and the digging of yams in the wrong season. Elsewhere secret or, more correctly, closed associations generally play an important part in social life as judicial bodies and in ritual matters.

As already stated, the lower and middle portions of the Senegal River form the ethnic divide between Hamites and Negroes. Immediately south of the river the latter are represented by the Wolof (or Jolof), who, with the Serer, occupy most of the territory between the Senegal and the Gambia Rivers. With these Senegalese must be included the Tukolor, and such Mandingo tribes as the Bambara and the Malinke, constituting a great group of dolichocephals, with a cephalic index of 74–75 and with generally broad noses (N.I. 93), though relatively narrow noses occasionally occur, perhaps due to miscegenation. Apart from the Serer, said to stand nearly 69 inches high, these tribes are generally only moderately tall, with a stature of about 67 inches. The Wolof, besides occupying the seaboard between St. Louis and Cape Verde (including Dakar) and the south bank of the Senegal, extend inland for a considerable distance. They are said to be the blackest and most garrulous of African peoples (their name being variously explained as meaning 'speaker' or 'black'). Most Wolof are nominally Muhammadan, a few Christian, but pagan rites are observed and offerings are made to household deities, the most popular, the lizard, having in many houses a bowl of milk set aside for it daily. The Wolof have three hereditary castes—nobles, craftsmen, and the despised musicians and slaves. The old kingdom of Cayor, the largest of the Wolof states, was preserved under French colonial rule, the king being elected from the royal family.

The country of the Serer, between the Gambia and Salum Rivers to the south of Cape Verde, formerly included territory east and north of their present home, so that they were at one time neighbours of the Tukolor, and formed part, with the Wolof, of their empire; the languages of the three peoples show many similarities and traces of borrowing. They have also mixed with Mandingo, from which people most of their ruling families come. The Serer have the reputation of being extraordinarily tall, but actual measurements hardly bear this out. They are less black than the Wolof, but have coarser features.

The Mandingo—more correctly Mande—constitute one of the most important groups of Senegal and West Sudan. They occupy most of the region between the Atlantic and the Upper Niger as far south as about latitude 9° N., and include such large and important tribes as the Dyula, Kassonke, Jallonke, Bambara (more correctly Banmana), Soninke, Malinke, and Vei. The typical Mandingo are described as tall and slender in build, with finer features, fuller beard, and lighter skin than the neighbouring populations; indeed it is claimed that they hold a position in the Western Sudan analogous to that of the Hausa in northern Nigeria and are thus destined to a position of increasing importance in the countries they inhabit. If this is so it constitutes an interesting example of time's revenges, for in the district of Manding, the original home of the Mande-speaking peoples, lies the site of the famous medieval city of Melle which, in the thirteenth century, and especially under Mansa-Musa (1311–31), became the capital of the most powerful Sudanese state of which there is authentic record. Only in 1500, when Melle was captured by the Songhai king, Omar Askia, did the Empire of Melle or Mali cease to exist.

The Bambara (or Banmana), besides having a clan organization, attach much importance to their castes or occupational guilds, such as the Semono (fishermen), Numu (smiths), etc.; these caste-names are found among other Mandingo people, who tend to be distinguished by their occupation-name rather than by that of their tribe. Some clans and even tribes are associated in a peculiar relationship commonly known to anthropologists as the 'joking relationship', in which, although bound to render each other assistance in case of need, the common manifestation of their alliance is the right to insult one another publicly—it might almost be said ceremonially—without giving offence.

Circumcision of boys and excision of girls is general, the operation being performed at about the age of ten, as among the Malinke, and only after this ceremony are the young people full members of the tribe. Both sexes go clothed, and tribal face-scars are found throughout the group.

The Bambara are essentially agriculturists, living in small villages, sometimes consisting of one family only, in cylinder-huts with conical straw roofs. In each community the religious and civil power is usually combined in one individual, the *dugutigi*, the 'master of the land', traditionally the descendant of the first settler, though in the case of recent migration he may be elected by the community. He is the high priest of the village, the one person who can propitiate the local spirits and by making them offerings obtain their goodwill and protection. The office is hereditary, in a patrilineal lineage, passing from brother to brother, and then to the eldest son. Although in some villages there may be a second chief for administrative and political purposes the power of the latter is purely civil, and the *dugutigi* remains supreme in all matters concerning the allotment of land, as well as in spiritual affairs.

The Bambara have been little affected by Islam and retain their animistic beliefs and ancestor worship. Each village has its presiding spirit (*dasiri*) or divine ancestor, usually resident in a tree, at which sacrifices are made and prayers offered by the *dugutigi* on all important occasions; conical altars of earth, on which is placed an earthen vessel, also serve as shrines. When the *dasiri* leaves his sacred tree he is thought not to set foot upon the ground but to mount a special animal—serpent, lizard, rat, donkey, or even goat—which, on account of its office, is also sacred, and is allowed to wander freely through the village helping itself to what it wants.

The Songhai dominion, despite the Moroccan conquest at the end of the sixteenth century, persisted until the French took Timbuktu; but the decline and fall of the kingdom did not greatly affect the two million folk constituting the Songhai nation and occupying the country along the eastern part of the great bend of the Niger. They are essentially Negroes who have absorbed much northern blood, yet in spite of miscegenation with Tuareg and Fulani they are in every respect one people, with a single speech and Islam as their religion. Physically, the Songhai are moderately tall, with a stature of about 68 inches. They are long-headed, with a cephalic index of 75·5, their northern blood being especially obvious in their relatively well-formed noses, which do not reach the lower limit of platyrrhiny, with an average nasal index of 84. Other evidence is to be found in their skin colour, which is described as coppery brown, never of the dark, almost black, colour of the Negroes of Dahomey and Ghana. Their hair, however, is always spiralled.

In continuity with the Songhai, and reaching to the head-waters of the Upper Volta, are the Mossi, Gurunsi, Tem, Barba or Borgu, and other similar tribes. Their chiefdoms, while they have to a considerable extent withstood Muhammadanism, have nevertheless been infiltrated by Fula, Songhai, and Hausa influence.

The Mossi comprise a large portion of the population of French-speaking West Africa, where they centre round Ouaga-dougou and extend into the north-west districts of Ghana. Their ruling families appear to have reached their present home in the basin of the Volta from the east, merging with the indigenous population and forming a homogeneous people so far as language and culture are concerned. In the middle of the fourteenth century Mossi, Dagomba, and Mamprussi were united under one leader and for a short time were in possession of Timbuktu. The government is centralized, and the districts with their villages are grouped into administrative or vassal provinces under chiefs appointed by the king, who resides at Ouagadougou with his ministers, consisting of the chiefs of the five provinces, and numerous hereditary court dignitaries.

The Mossi are agriculturists, with millet as the staple crop. They possess few cattle, but good horses and many donkeys. They are pagans: ancestor worship plays a large part in their religion and sacrifices are offered in sacred groves to both ancestors and the Earth. They have an esoteric cult of the Sun and Moon practised by a religious fraternity wearing masks, and the priests of this cult throughout the year tend the sacred fire, kept alight in a small recess in the wall of their hut and associated with a (new-fire?) ceremony at the end of the rains.

To the south of the Mossi are the Gurunsi (Grunshi), a general term given by the Mossi to a large congeries of closely related tribes typified by the Kassena, Nankani, Tallensi, etc., all speaking dialects related to that of the Mossi, whom they also resemble in many ways in their mode of life.

Among all these tribes there is the institution of the 'father' or 'master' of the land, already described among the Bambara (p. 36). This is a ritual office connected with the cult of the Earth, which is widespread throughout West Africa but has in this and other regions been pushed into the background by individual groups claiming secular superiority. The localized patrilineal clan is the sovereign political unit in this area, there being no tribal chiefs. A supreme deity associated with the Sun, as well as the Earth, lineage and family ancestors, and numerous magical fetishes, make up the religious system common to the area.

In the Central Sudan east of the Niger the advance of Islam has swept away or greatly modified the aborigines except along a southern fringe and in a few parts of the Chad basin. The older tribal organization has been overlain by states, and for nearly a thousand years the Central Sudan has been occupied by muhammadanized peoples gathered together into political systems of some permanence, each with its own language and each to a considerable extent developing a tradition of its own. The Songhai Empire has already been mentioned, and to this might be added the Kingdoms of Bornu, Kanem, and Baghirmi, while the Hausa, on account of their importance in Nigeria, will be described later in more detail. The Kanembu (the people of Kanem), the Kanuri (of Bornu), and the Baghirmi cluster round Lake Chad, and here too survive such pagan 'aboriginals' as the Buduma of Lake

Chad, the Mosgu, and the Mandara, who inhabit the swampy region of the Shari basin. The Kanembu (the Beriberi of the Hausa) have no doubt been considerably berberized, and are perhaps to be related also to the Tibu (p. 96), while the Kanuri of Bornu appear to be more distinctly arabized, perhaps with some admixture of Fulani blood.

In this group we are again dealing with broad-nosed dolichocephals, somewhat longer-headed, it would seem, than the Senegalese group: e.g. the Kanembu have a cephalic index of 73 and a stature of nearly 66 inches, while the pagan Buduma of Lake Chad, who have been considered facially to resemble such Nilotes as the Shilluk (p. 112), are some two inches taller with a cephalic index of nearly 74.

Little is known of the history of the Felup, more correctly Dyola, a coastal tribe of obscure origin who have spread at the expense of their neighbours from Gambia to the Bissagos Islands. Their name has been used by the Portuguese for a congeries of tribes who fell under their influence, even though some of them have later become Muhammadans. The Felup are described as typical Negroes, with a matrilineal organization, and as worshipping a god associated with the firmament and rain.

In Sierra Leone and Liberia the Mende and Kpelle (Mandingo group), Temne, Bulom, Kissi, and Gola are perhaps the most important tribes. The Bulom have achieved some notoriety as the alleged originators of the powerful Poro society, referred to on p. 33.

The Kru are a group of kindred tribes in Liberia and the Ivory Coast. They probably number about 200,000 altogether. Their languages form a distinct group, which gives no justification for traditions of origin from the interior. The coastal Kru have long been noted as brave and skilful seamen and fishermen, and are to be found on almost every ship trading on the Guinea Coast. Typically Negro in features, they are of exceptionally fine physique, and are said to be particularly intelligent and enterprising. The Kru are divided into small commonwealths, each with an hereditary chief, and have a well-marked system of age-grades. There are also secret societies for magico-religious and judicial purposes, one of the chief being the *Kwi-Iru* ('children of departed spirits'), open to all males except the very young, and presided over by a masked 'father'.

The Guinea Coast is portioned out amongst tribes speaking languages of the extensive Kwa division of the Sudanic language family. Though not mutually intelligible, these languages have a common basis, being notable for the use of both semantic and grammatical tones. Dialects of the Akan branch of the Kwa division are spoken by the Ashanti, Fanti, and many smaller tribes of Ghana and the Ivory Coast, numbering probably two million people altogether. Going eastwards we find the Ewe cluster, which includes the languages spoken in Dahomey, and the related Yoruba cluster spoken by more than three million people in southern Nigeria. The Nupe of central Nigeria and the numerous more or less independent tribes and communities of Ibo, Ibibio, Efik, and their congeners of south-eastern Nigeria fall into this group.

The Guinea Coast is notable for the number of relatively highly organized nation-states, such as Ashanti, Dahomey, the Yoruba kingdoms, Benin and Nupe, which have arisen in the area. The early European travellers were much impressed by the barbaric splendour of the royal courts of these states and gave lurid accounts of the practice of human sacrifice on a great scale, at the time of their annual harvest festivals, in Ashanti, Dahomey, and Benin. Close study by Rattray and other anthropologists has shown that, atrocious as these practices seemed to their first European witnesses, they are no criterion of the political, religious, and moral abilities and qualities of these nations, who are today among the most progressive peoples in Africa, being specially zealous in education, trade, and government.

Traditionally, these states all had elaborate military organizations, and highly developed legal systems based on a hierarchy of local and regional councils acting as both administrative and judicial bodies and culminating in the king's court. They had quite complex bodies of public and private law. A somewhat shadowy High God is associated with the worship of numerous lesser gods and quasi-mythological deified heroes, often connected with natural phenomena of social significance (e.g. rivers and lakes, smallpox, thunder and lightning), and in the eastern areas sometimes forming the focal points of secret cults and societies. The splendid art of Benin and the Yoruba areas is well known. All through the area, however, craftsmanship in wood, textiles, gold, and bronze was very highly developed, being carried on by guilds or in specialized villages giving hereditary craft service to the courts. Trade was highly developed among them, partly under the direction of rulers and in the national interest. A characteristic article traded to the interior in exchange for cloth, livestock, slaves, etc., was the kola-nut. Trade with the coastal ports played a very important part in their history. Gold and slaves were the main items exchanged for firearms, gin, textiles, and other products of Europe.

Of these pyramidally organized states Ashanti was until recently ethnologically the best known, owing to the researches of R. S. Rattray. His anthropometric measurements suggest that the Ashanti are a particularly homogeneous people in their ethnic make-up. This may be true of those parts of Ashanti which were relatively secluded between the sea and the rain forest, being thus protected from the pressure of northern peoples with much admixture of Fulani and other light-coloured non-Negro stocks. Of moderate stature (men average 64·5 inches, women 60·5 inches) and slight build, they tend to have the very dark skin, relatively broad nose (index—male average 95, female 90), and long head, characteristic of the true Negro stock.

Culturally the Ashanti are typical in every respect of the Akan-speaking peoples, differing only in the exceptional degree to which they have developed the characteristic Akan political institutions. The basis of Akan social organization is the rule of matrilineal descent. Every freeborn Akan, whatever his tribe, belongs to one of eight exogamous matrilineal clans, each associated with a totemic animal connected with the first emergence of the clan ancestress on earth. Some secrecy surrounds these totem animals, but children are taught to respect them.

While inheritance of property and succession to chiefship and other offices and ranks are determined by matrilineal descent, paternity is specially important in Akan social organization.

Through his father every person is a member of a ritual group (*ntoro*) of patrilineally connected people. There are about twelve of these *ntoro* groups dispersed, like the clans, throughout the country. Each *ntoro* has one or more mythical animal ancestors and if one of these animals (e.g. python or leopard) is found dead members of the appropriate *ntoro* bury it and put on mourning-signs. Marriage is prohibited between near *ntoro* kin. In Ashanti, it is believed that a child derives his blood and body from his mother and his personality as a spiritual essence from his father, this being connected with his *ntoro* group. Each group is believed to have distinct personality traits, e.g. aggressiveness, kindliness, etc.

Neither clans nor *ntoro* groups ever act as units on a tribal basis. Such action occurs only in the local divisions of a clan. These consist of matrilineal lineages of eight to twelve genera-tions of acknowledged common descent, whose members live close together, have a common 'stool-house' in which the conse-crated stools of their forebears are preserved and given sacrifices and libations at *Adae* festivals, bury their dead in the private cemetery, and in particular have a male head who, with the assistance of the elders and a female head, exercises oversight over the affairs of the lineage. All political offices, from the kingship down, are hereditary in particular lineages of the community in which the office is exercised. Thus the kingship is vested in a lineage of the Oyoko clan domiciled in Kumasi. Land and other property rights are generally vested in segments of these local lineages. Sexual relations between members of the same lineage are incestuous and were formerly punished by execution.

In Ashanti, with a population of rather over half a million, (as among the Twi-speaking peoples generally) the king was para-mount lord over a confederation of provincial chiefs and received levies and occasional tribute from them, the chiefs in their turn exercising authority over the sub-chiefs and headmen of the villages under their jurisdiction. Besides ruling as suzerain the king himself exercised the functions of a provincial chief so far as concerned the affairs of the capital and the villages dependent on it. Each provincial chief was semi-independent, living in regal state in his capital, where he dispensed justice in his own local court, but except in the case of slaves the king alone could order capital punishment. The king was not an absolute monarch, but was controlled to a certain extent by his council, composed of the queen-mother (who was the second person in the kingdom), the chiefs of the most important provinces, and the general of the army, and this council had to be consulted on all matters of external policy. The government was thus rather that of an aristo-cracy than a personal despotism, apart from the power of the king to inflict capital punishment for crime or treason. The military organization was by local areas, generally into two companies with hereditary captains owing allegiance to their provincial chiefs. Each company was known by a distinct title, usually derived from the town-quarter of its members. In the Fanti towns the rivalry between the various companies was so keen that the flaunting of a company flag in a quarter belonging to another company would generally lead to serious disturbance. In Ashanti the paramount interests of the nation prevailed over such factional conflicts.

The royal stool of Ashanti—the well-known 'Golden Stool'—came into being during the time of Osai Tutu (1700–30), the fourth known king of Ashanti and the founder of the Empire. In the early years of his reign a man named Anotchi arrived in the country and announced that he had a mission from the Sky God to make Ashanti a great and powerful nation. A great gathering was summoned in Kumasi, and while the air was thick with dust and the heavens terrible with thunder, Anotchi drew down from the sky a wooden stool, partly covered with gold. This stool did not fall to earth, but descended slowly upon the knees of Osai Tutu, to whom and to whose people Anotchi proclaimed that the stool contained the *sunsum* or soul of the Ashanti nation, that their power, their health, and their bravery and welfare were in this stool, and that if it were destroyed then the Ashanti nation would sicken and lose its vitality and power. The stool is said never to have touched the ground, nor did any mortal ever sit upon it, and when it was taken to Bantama once every year it was con-veyed under its own umbrella and surrounded by resplendent attendants.

That the Golden Stool should be regarded as the palladium of the realm is entirely in accord with African politico-ritual

C

concepts (for another example cf. p. 115, where the stool of Nyakang of the Shilluk is described), for in Ashanti each chief has a stool, supposed to be the respository of it's owner's soul, and fetters are placed round the central support of the stool 'to bind the soul to it'. After the death of a wise chief his stool is blackened with soot and yolk of egg and is deposited in the stool-house with those of his ancestors, thus becoming a shrine which the departed spirit may be called upon to enter on special occasions to receive adulation and gifts. Thus in the *Adae* ceremony, a rite observed throughout Ashanti twice in every successive forty-three days, the spirits of the departed clan-chiefs are propitiated and their favours solicited. The chief sacrifices a sheep in the stool-house, the blood is smeared on the stools, and a piece of meat placed on each, with a prayer for long life and prosperity, while the minstrels drone the names and attributes of the dead. At this ceremony yams are also offered, and a little rum is poured on each stool.

The Ashanti acknowledge an Earth spirit, and Nyame, the supreme god in the firmament, a remote being whose cult plays little part in the everyday life of the people. From him are derived numerous lesser gods (*obosom*)—of whom the most important is Tano—graded in a descending scale until they reach or almost merge into the class called *suman*, who are among the lowest rank of supernatural powers. But although *suman* and other spiritual agencies are propitiated, by far the most essential, the real working part of Ashanti religion is a cult of the dead, including dead kings, the most important of all rites being the great festival of the dead, generally (but incorrectly) known to Europeans as the 'Yam Custom'. This ceremony was the occasion of sacrifice to the ghosts of the kings, wine and new yams being offered to them by the king with these words:

The edges of the years have met; I take sheep and new yams and give you that you may eat.
Life to me.
Life to this my Ashanti people.
Women who cultivate the farms, when they do so grant the food comes forth in abundance.
Do not allow any illness to come.

Only after the spirits had partaken of the new crops might the king and nation eat of them.

The proper title of the ceremony is *Odwira* (*dwira*, to purify, to cleanse), and though uninitiated spectators have laid stress on the amount of intoxicating liquor drunk and of human blood spilt, these features were but incidental to its real purpose. Our best authority describes the rite as 'an annual ceremony held in September in honour and propitiation of the Ashanti kings who "had gone elsewhere", and for the cleansing of the whole nation from defilement . . . a feast of the dead, very closely associated with the crops and the first-fruits . . . hence the [European] name "Yam Custom", by which this ceremony has hitherto been universally described. . . . Not only was it a cleansing of the nation, but the purification of shrines of ancestral spirits, of the gods, and of lesser non-human spirits.' He emphasizes the political significance and practical unity of the rite (now no longer held) and its magico-religious aspect, which by entailing the annual presence and participation of the tributary chiefs, served as a guarantee of their loyalty and helped to bring cohesion to the many loosely bound factions owning allegiance to the Ashanti king.

The 'Yam Custom' was witnessed by Bowdich in 1817 and he has described it in realistic terms, illustrating his description with a most vivid coloured plate.[1]

In Dahomey the king and the royal clan had more autocratic powers than in Ashanti. The death of the king was the signal for the women of the palace to destroy furniture and utensils and then to kill themselves, that they might at once join their lord with his belongings. At the death of Andázu II in 1789, 595 of these women are said to have perished, in addition to a suitable following of soldiers, Amazons, eunuchs, bards, etc. The annual 'Custom', a continuation of the Grand Customs performed at the death of a king, periodically increased the retinue of the departed monarch in the spirit world. Like the Ashanti 'Yam Custom', the annual Custom served a political end, the presence of the chiefs being required at the capital. Hundreds of victims also perished yearly as the result of the rule that every act

[1] T. E. Bowdich, *Mission from Cape Coast Castle to Ashantee* (1819).

performed by the king must be reported by a messenger to the other world, the message being given to a captive, carefully gagged, who was decapitated after having received a coin and a bottle of rum for the expenses of the journey.

An institution peculiar to Dahomey was the corps of female soldiery, called Amazons by Europeans and known in Dahomey as the 'King's wives' and 'our mothers'. Sir Richard Burton, who in 1862 saw the army march out of Kana on a military expedition, computed the number of female troops at 2,500 (of whom one-third were unarmed), and attributed the origin of the corps to the masculine physique of the Dahoman women which enabled them to compete with men in enduring toil, hardship, and privations. Originally the Amazons consisted mainly of criminals, wives detected in adultery and women who had been sent to the king as worthy of death for some misdemeanour, and had been drafted into the army instead of being sacrificed at the 'Customs', for which criminals were reserved. Under Gezo (1818) the force was reorganized and greatly enlarged, and his successor Gelele had every girl brought to him before marriage and enrolled those who pleased him. The women were sworn to celibacy, though the king had the privilege of taking any of them to wife; they had the status of king's wives and could not be touched without danger of death. A particular fetish placed at the palace gate was said to cause pregnancy in all who had been unchaste. In theory they only saw members of the opposite sex when on the march or in the field, and on parade the two sexes were separated by strips of bamboo laid on the ground. But in spite of these precautions, during Burton's visit no fewer than 150 Amazons were found pregnant and brought to justice with their lovers, some being condemned to death. Such women were executed by their own sex within the palace walls.

The Amazons were armed with blunderbusses, muskets, and long razor-shaped knives with 18-inch blades. They formed the king's bodyguard, and in time of peace one of their duties was to accompany the women of the palace when they went to the well for water, the party being preceded by a bell which was the signal for all men to get out of their path. During the 'Customs', reviews and manoeuvres were frequently held, in which the Amazons took a prominent part, and M. Borghero, who in 1861 witnessed one of these combats, writes of how the bare-footed female warriors were ordered to charge over a bank of thorny acacias and escalade a house covered with a bed of the same thorns, a feat which they accomplished with the utmost dash, dragging back their prisoners to the feet of the king. In battle the Amazons were said to display a ferocious courage; their chief aim was to carry off trophies of their prowess in the shape of banners and human heads and jawbones, the latter being prized for the ornamentation of drums, etc., and frequently torn from the wounded and living foe. Burton, however, was not impressed by the Amazons:

They manoeuvre with the precision of a flock of sheep . . . and though affecting a military swagger, their faces are anything but ferocious. . . . The officers, distinguished by their white head-cloths, and by an esquiress-at-arms, generally a small slave girl, carrying a musket, led their commands. They were mostly remarkable for a stupendous steatopygy, and for a development of adipose tissue which suggested anything but ancient virginity.

According to their traditions, the population of Dahomey are of very mixed origins and this appears to be confirmed in their physical characters. Some of the tribes in the north who were conquered by the ruling aristocracy clearly belong to the great congeries of small, very primitive 'remnant' tribes of negroid cultivators which stretches across the Sudan from West Africa to the Nuba Hills (see p. 54).

The Yoruba have a cephalic index of nearly 76, which differs but little from those of other Guinea tribes, such as the Ibo with an index rather over 76 and the Ibibio (including Efik) with one of 75, though the Ijaw (or Calabar) have an index approaching 78. The Yoruba, although now occupying a considerable area on the coast, are really an inland people. The Ilorin district of northern Nigeria, only comparatively recently islamized, marks the limits of their culture. They are known to be among the most advanced of the West African peoples.

With their common religious centre in what they regard as their place of origin, the town of Ife, and belief in descent from a single culture hero, they have a marked degree of cultural uniformity. The local community is based on patrilineal descent groups. Chiefs, aided by partly hereditary, partly appointed councils, have great authority. This conduces to the security of life and property and has no doubt contributed to the creation of the large towns that are distinctive of Yoruba social life, though intestine wars and the great trading skill of the people also played a part in this. Yoruba religion is of great complexity as it includes both an elaborate ancestor cult, and the worship of a Sky God, Olorun, and of lesser gods such as Shango, the God of Thunder, that are virtually local gods. Secret societies of men and women, especially the well-known Ogboni society, had judicial functions in maintaining law and order.

4

The True Negro (*continued*)

FOR THE LAST TWENTY PAGES we have been occupied with the tribes of the coastal zone, extending first south and then east from Cape Verde to the Cameroons, a region of swamp, mangroves, and dense forest, with heavy rainfall and almost continuous humidity. Apart from disturbing factors necessarily existing in the neighbourhood of such great rivers as the Niger and Benue, the hinterland becomes progressively less difficult, open forest and 'park' country giving place to poor steppe and even semi-desert conditions along the northern borders of the northern territories of the countries of the West African coastline, so that the conditions of land and climate gradually approximate to those of the Sudan and allow of a modification of the inhabitants due to the infusion of 'European' blood.

Here, occupying the northern areas of Ghana and Nigeria, as well as the hinterland of the Ivory Coast and Guinea, are innumerable pagan tribes whose population totals several millions. Most of them are poor in material culture and the only form of government is that of clan heads and priests of the Earth. It is in their territories that the Muhammadan Fulani Emirates and Hausa kingdoms rose to power. In these northern territories it is necessary to bear in mind not only the possible fundamental unity of the black hillmen stretching westwards from Kordofan and Darfur, but also to remember the series of Muhammadan kingdoms which in medieval times spread across Africa from the Nile to the Senegal, for these two factors constitute the background of the present tribal groupings and cultures.

The sketch map on p. 9 f. showing the main trade routes from the north will give some idea of the possibilities of indirect contact with the Mediterranean cultures, a matter scarcely explored as yet; it also gives some idea of the main paths of the slave traffic along which Negro racial strains entered into Mediterranean Africa before the medieval opening of the sea route to West Africa.

The Fulani, because of their Hamitic origin and culture (though they are steadily absorbing more and more Negro blood), are described in Chapter 6. The Hausa, on the other hand, are essentially Negro, though they speak a Hamitic language. They must not, however, be regarded as a single race or stock: rather are they people of diverse origin now united in speaking a Hamitic language but recruited over centuries from neighbouring tribes. The position will be clear if it is realized that the term 'Hausa' is used to denote (a) the Hausa language, (b) the country where the main body of the Hausa-speaking peoples are centred (i.e. from Zaria to Katsina and Sokoto), and (c) as Hausawa, all those peoples of the Central and Western Sudan who speak the Hausa language as their mother tongue. Primarily, therefore, the term, like 'Bantu', is linguistic, but also to a considerable extent religious and cultural, being applied to tribes differing widely in racial characteristics. It should not be confused with the term 'Habe', used by the Fulani of Kano and Sokoto when referring to those with no Fulani blood, whether pagan or Muslim and whether or not they are Hausa-speaking. In spite of the mixed origin of the nation there is nevertheless a basic distinguishing element in the Negroid Hausa:

The typical Hausa is very black, like most of the central Sudanese; he is essentially long-headed, and the skull frequently has a pentagonal appearance; he is markedly less prognathous, less platyrrhine, and less muscular than the West Coast Negro, but is taller, having great length of leg. . . . In character he is much franker and less suspicious than the Fula; is more cheerful and has a keener sense of humour than the Yoruba.

Numbering about eight million the Hausa are centred principally in the Muslim Emirates of Sokoto, Katsina, Kano, and Zaria, but Hausa towns are found in all the provinces of northern Nigeria, and socially and economically they may be said to dominate the area, constituting more than one-third of the total population. They are in general excellent farmers and rearers of stock, enterprising traders and skilful artisans, having developed a variety of industries such as leatherwork and cloth mats; as carriers they show remarkable strength and endurance, and under British leadership proved fearless fighters. Islam, with the Sultan of Sokoto as spiritual chief, is the religion of the majority of the inhabitants of Hausaland, although some Hausa-speaking tribes, e.g. Abagwariga and Maguzawa, are pagan.

In the Middle Ages the Hausa, though never a conquering group, attained great political power. They were then divided into seven states, known as the Hausa Bokwoi (seven Hausa), named Kano, Zaria, Daura, Gobir, Katsina, Biram, and Rano, after the sons of their legendary founder. This confederation extended its authority over many of the neighbouring countries and remained paramount until its conquest by the Fulani in the first decade of the nineteenth century. According to tradition the progenitor of the kings of the Hausa states was one Abayejidu, son of the King of Baghdad, who came with his followers to Daura, where the ruler was Daurama, ninth of a succession of queens. On his arrival Abayejidu, being thirsty, asked for water, and when told that the well was guarded by a serpent called Ki Sarki, who prevented the drawing of water, slew the reptile and cut off its head, the queen in her gratitude marrying him. After this the people of Daura spoke no longer of the queen, but of Mai-Kai-Sarki ('the man who killed Sarki'), and henceforth Sarki came to mean king or chieftain in the Hausa language. This legend is recorded as an example of the Hausa tendency to borrow and greatly exaggerate Eastern connexions, due to the increasing prestige and pressure of Islam.

After the Fulani conquest the Hausa states were ruled by highly centralized administrations under somewhat autocratic chiefs in a feudal type of social and political organization. But the aboriginal forms of domestic organization and vestiges of pagan custom and belief have survived.

These resemble the customs and beliefs of the many surviving independent pagan tribes of this part of the hinterland, some very small, others relatively large, and including the Jar, Jukun, Angas, Gwari, Birom, Tiv, etc. The Nupe (related to the Gwari) are an important mixed Muslim-pagan tribe in Niger province, with a Hausa-like political and economic system. Of few of these people have we precise knowledge. Save in Nupe, no strong native states or kingdoms seem to have arisen here as they have in the south; rather it seems that throughout a great part of northern Nigeria the social organization is essentially that of a number of villages united into a single community, and this 'consolidated group', as Meek calls it, may be coterminous with a tribe or a section of a tribe. But throughout this form of political grouping it is generally possible to discover a unifying influence arising from a sense of kinship, and therefore the possession of a common religious cult intensified by pressure from without. Thus the Warjawa of northern Nigeria have seen headmen of sections or sub-tribes acknowledging the authority of a chief, who actually has little civil power though it seems that in war he would act as leader. Much the same organization is found in many of the larger tribes, such as the Birom, where the chief is little more than suzerain of the local groups, and sometimes, as among the Angas, derives almost the whole of his authority from his position as religious head, though it is true that he has certain prerogatives such as hunting dues and a proportion of the slaves captured in war.

It is in some such loose organization as we have sketched that in this part of Africa paramount chiefs may arise, when a strong man or war leader begins to extend his power beyond his own group, thus originating loose confederacies, which in face of a hostile attack are welded into something approaching a small nation. Such a man was the paramount chief of Bede, who won his position when standing against Fulani and Bornu aggression; he then, it is said, made sure of the position for himself and his descendants by removing the important men of the minor groups acknowledging his authority.

Of these tribes the Tiv are the largest, numbering about 800,000. They speak a semi-Bantu language, and have no indigenous chiefs but are organized in a lineage system based on the principle of segmental opposition. They are vigorous and warlike, and noted for their complex system of marriage by exchange and for their intricate ideas on witchcraft.

On the cultural side almost the whole of northern Nigeria is patrilineal, the exceptions being in the south-east of the area, where a number of tribes are matrilineal. A curious feature is the existence among them of unusual and elaborate marriage customs, in some cases like a mingling of polyandry and polygyny. The Jukun, to whom reference is made below, were claimed by Meek to have been matrilineal until recent years.

Belief in a supreme being residing in the sky or, as among the Jukun, identified with the sun, is common among these pagan tribes. Ancestor worship, and a great variety of spirit or animistic cults, also occur.

Circumcision, universal among Islamic tribes, is also practised by most pagans, though groups that circumcise and groups that do not may be found within the limits of a single tribe; the Tiv appear to have taken to circumcision fairly recently. Among the pagan tribes, except the Tiv, circumcision is sometimes part of a series of initiation ceremonies in which the boys are instructed in the lore of the tribe and taught to be obedient to the old men, corporal punishment being frequently administered during this period. Often the rites are concluded by taking the lads to a shrine and showing them certain sacred symbols. Among the Jukun the novices were led in blindfold; the bandage was suddenly removed and the initiates were asked what they could see. The correct answer was 'Nothing at all', and it was said that if any novice lost his self-possession and named the sacred objects he was forthwith put to death, for one so lacking in discretion could not be trusted with the tribal secrets. Clitoridectomy and excision of the *labia* is also practised among some tribes in northern Nigeria, as it is among the Mandingo of Senegal and the Yoruba and Bini of southern Nigeria.

The Jukun are among the most interesting, and smallest, of the pagan peoples of West Africa. The most striking of their social features is the semi-divine character of the king: he must not touch the ground with his hands or uncovered feet lest the crops be ruined, while until recently he is said to have been ceremonially slain at the harvest festival at the end of seven years' reign, a festival which the king during colonial rule refused to hold, lest in spite of European influence he should go the way of his fathers. But although the belief in the power of the king to control the rain, and hence fertility, conferred on the monarch a position of unquestioned authority, actual administration was largely in the hands of members of the royal family; in fact there was more bureaucracy among the Jukun than among other pagan tribes of Nigeria. They have, indeed, no subjects. Especially important positions were held at the Jukun court by two women, one of whom was sister in the classificatory sense of the last king and was ruler of the palace women, while her colleague was the favourite wife of the deceased monarch and was thus the reigning sovereign's official 'mother' (cf. Ashanti). The king consulted her on all important matters, and she had the right to offer asylum to fugitives from justice. It was these two women who virtually controlled the election of the new king.

So far we have dealt with the true West African Negro and with tribes which in the present stage of our knowledge may be regarded as closely akin. Besides these there are a number of black-skinned, spiral-haired peoples who although differing from the West African Negro are scarcely to be regarded as having arisen from a mixture of Negro and Berber. One such stock is represented by the Nuba of southern Kordofan, a country presenting in the main a great plain dotted with isolated hills and ranges. At the present day the Nuba are essentially hill people, though it is likely that Arab pressure may have played a part in driving them from the plains. Linguistically the Nuba of the more southern hills are particularly interesting as speaking a language which has been termed 'Bantoid', i.e. a language which although not Bantu has alliterative concordance and perhaps an approach to noun classes, thus differing entirely from the Sudanic and hamiticized (Nubian) languages spoken by the more northern non-Arab inhabitants of Kordofan.

Physically the southern Nuba are tall men, with an average stature of about 68 inches, and a cephalic index of 76 to 77. Culturally they show considerable variety. Men mostly go naked, but women wear leaves, fibre aprons, or bristles of dried grass.

Circumcision of men and mutilation of girls are rare, but cicatrization is widely practised. House forms again vary widely. If an attempt be made to relate the Nuba to other peoples, the relationship should be sought in the south, perhaps with the Bari-speaking tribes of the west band (p. 109) or in the far west with the black hillmen of the northern provinces of Nigeria and the north of Ghana (p. 47); it is probably no accident that the cicatrices of the Nuba women, the quartz ornaments they sometimes wear in the lower lip, and the unusual structure of the houses in certain parts of Nuba country, can be closely paralleled in these western areas. Actually we know that people resembling the Nuba inhabit the hills of Darfur, extending as far west as Wadai, so that there is nothing inherently improbable in seeking to carry the relationship still farther west.

It is probable then that many of the other non-Arab races of Darfur and Wadai are largely of the same stock as the Nuba, though in many instances there has been an infusion of Arab and Hamitic blood. This is specially true of the Tungur and Dargu, two ancient peoples of Darfur; while of the Fur themselves, the people from whom the country takes its name, it is known that they descended from the hills of Jebel Marra in the sixteenth century, so that it is extremely likely that they too were in origin of Nuba stock; indeed, though nominally Muhammadans, they still have a stone and tree cult so persistent that particular places associated with rocks and trees are regarded as shrines, the local spirit being envisaged as existing in snake form, just as on one of the Nuba hills in southern Kordofan. The Sultanate of Darfur, which continued to exist until the revolt of the Sultan during the first world war led to his downfall, was interesting as the last of the hybrid but predominantly Negro states which at one time stretched across Africa north of the forest zone. In spite of the Muhammadanism of its ruling class it was administered rather on the model of an advanced Negro society such as that of the Bushongo (p. 134) than on an Arabic model. It is not, however, suggested that there was any direct connexion between Darfur and the Congo.

East of Kordofan, Dar Fung, the country between the White and Blue Niles, is inhabited by a number of tribes—Berta,

Hameg, etc.—of the same stock as the Nuba, though some of them have been considerably arabized. Their more Negro representatives probably link up with such Shankalla tribes (p. 72) as the Kunam and Barea of the Ethiopian borderlands. In the south-eastern corner of Dar Fung and on the Sobat River are the Burun, tall, almost brachycephalic Negroes, of whose social organization we know nothing.

Another group of Negroes to whom reference must be made are the non-Bantu tribes of the area between the Nile and the Congo and extending westwards north of the Uele, thus occupying much of the Ubangi-Uele basin. Here is a group of little-known tribes, including many of the 'High Nilotic' group of Westermann (p. 111), speaking Sudanic languages, and whose physical characters seem to mark them off both from the Nilotes and from their Bantu-speaking neighbours in the south. They are essentially mesocephals, perhaps reaching the lower grades of brachycephaly, relatively short in stature, generally thoroughly Negro in physiognomy, and—though there are exceptions—with a skin which is dark reddish-brown rather than 'black'. On the cultural side their peculiarities are most readily appreciated by contrasting them with the Nilotes, as in the following table:

NILOTES	MESOCEPHALIC GROUP
Herdsmen; cattle are extensively owned and are of the highest importance; barely enough grain is grown to feed the people and make beer.	Agriculturists; cultivation the chief occupation of the people, and with poultry-rearing provides food and interest; cattle not kept.
No cannibalism; human sacrifice very rare or absent.	Many tribes cannibalistic; human sacrifice common.
Men go naked, or with a skin suspended over the shoulders; hair of the head often worked up into an elaborate headdress.	Men clothed with a loin-cloth, or a bark-cloth garment sometimes almost amounting to trousers; hair plaited in lines down the side of the skull and (often) worked into 'pom-poms' at the end of each plait; hats of woven grass, sometimes decorated with a bunch of cock's feathers.

NILOTES

MESOCEPHALIC GROUP

Women wear a leather petticoat from waist to knee in front and behind.

Women (typically) wear a bunch of fresh leaves suspended in front and behind from a waistcord; sometimes an apron.

Ivory bracelets are worn on the upper arm.

Ivory bracelets not often seen.

To the mesocephals belong such tribes as the Bongo, the Jur (non-Shilluk-speaking), the Ndogo, the Azande—though as will be seen, this term denotes a highly composite people rather than a tribe—the Lendu, Mamvu, Kaliko, Mangbetu, Abarambo, etc. Of all these the Azande are the least unknown and may be taken as representing this group, though they are no doubt far more vigorous and intelligent than the majority of the peoples just mentioned. They differ moreover from the great majority of tribes of the Sudan and Congo in that they may fairly be regarded as a nation, for they are really a confederation of tribes under a supreme head, or sultan, belonging to a special ruling class, each tribe with its territorial sections and chiefs. The ruling class, known as the Avungara, is often, but probably inaccurately, stated to consist of descendants of one Gura, the ruler of a tribe or clan which some 200 years ago began a process of conquering and absorbing the neighbouring tribes. Actually at the time of the resettlement of the Sudan and of the occupation of the Congo by the Belgians the Azande confederation was pushing both east and west; it had crossed the Congo-Nile divide into the Sudan and was rapidly eating up the great majority of the mesocephalic tribes on the northern-flowing affluents of the Bahr-el-Ghazal. It is a matter for speculation what would have happened if it had reached the more open grass country inhabited by the pastoral Nilotes; certainly its onset would have been by far the sternest test to which the Nilotes have been subjected within the last few hundred years.

On account of the numerous peoples that go to constitute the Azande nation, skin-colour and measurements necessarily vary; indeed the reddish tinge of many Azande has been though to betoken Hamitic blood. A group measured in the Sudan gave a cephalic index of 79, with a stature of 65 inches; a larger group measured in the Congo an index of nearly two units lower and a stature which in some small sub-groups reached 69 inches.

Among most of these mesocephalic tribes the lower incisors are not removed, but some file the upper incisors to a point, as do the Makaraka, a V-shaped notch being filed between the central incisors.

The Azande have a clan organization. There are many clans, though these have no political, economic, or ceremonial functions; they are however totemic, and at death one soul is believed to pass into the totemic animal while another soul remains in the vicinity of the grave and later goes to join the ancestral spirits near the head-waters of streams. These spirits are the chief agencies worshipped, each homestead having a shrine at which offerings are made. A supreme being, Mbole, is recognized, but it seems that he is not invoked, except during periods of drought.

Leadership, both supreme, provincial, and even district, is limited to the Avungara, the political organization of the country consisting of a paramount chief ruling over a tribe, generally defined by river boundaries, with under him brothers and sons administering provinces, and commoners to act as deputies when desirable.

The Azande now circumcise almost universally, but this appears to be a new practice; it certainly is so in that part of the tribe in the Sudan, where the boys spend some six months in a special camp in the bush while they undergo instruction by the older men. There are a number of secret societies, mostly with a wide membership, since the entrance fees are small and there is usually no sex restriction. Little is known about them, but it seems that one of their main purposes is the practice of magic. The Azande appear to be the most eastern tribe who practise the poison-wood ordeal, the actual poison being usually administered to fowls and addressed when in the body of the fowl as a personal entity.

Finally, under the heading 'Negro', attention must be drawn to a little-known people scattered over the northern and central regions of South-West Africa, often described with the Hottentots because they have taken over many cultural characters from the latter. The Bergdama or Haukhoin (a pejorative term equivalent to 'dung people'), more correctly the =|=nu Khoin, 'black people', are included in this chapter since they appear to be a group of true Negroes long isolated from others of their stock. They are described as strong, heavily built men of medium height, very dark-skinned, with long heads, prognathism, and platyrrhiny. They speak the language of the Naman group of Hottentots, to whom they have long lived in subjection, and like the Bushmen they do not cultivate but live by hunting and on the wild vegetable produce of their country. The social unit is the patriarchal family, sometimes strengthened by more distant relatives and adherents too weak to fend for themselves. On the other hand, the ceremonial side of their lives seems to have been influenced by Bantu as well as by Hottentots. Thus, although they speak of a supreme spiritual being, ‖gauab, who is also found among the northern Bushmen and the Hottentots, they have in addition the sacred fire which is so important a feature of the neighbouring Bantu tribes, the Herero and Ambo:

Each little group has a sacred fire which must never be allowed to go out, but which must be guarded day and night by the chief wife of the patriarch. Day by day when the members of the group go out to seek for food the head of the group and the old men sit guarding the fire, and as long as that is aglow and respected by all, the hunters and collectors will find food for the day. All game must be laid by the sacred fire, and certain portions of it must be eaten ceremonially by the elders of the group. Each kind of berry and root, as it ripens, must be brought to the sacred fire before it can be eaten. All good, all evil hangs upon the guarding of the fire from all impurities, which come from breaches in the regulations as laid down in the traditions of the tribe.

At the present time there may be some twenty-nine thousand Bergdama in South-West Africa. In the old days they were essentially mountain people, but it was hardly from choice that they lived there; rather they were driven into the hills by the Herero, who killed them ruthlessly or at best made slaves of their young people, while the Hottentots, having obtained firearms, exterminated whole groups.

Many Bergdama are short and thickset, and one group in the Otavi highlands are strikingly small. The skull is generally long, with a low receding forehead, though some have a high and straight brow, a feature admired and praised in the old songs as resembling the high brow of the wild ox; the nose is broad with sunken nostrils, but the occasional appearance of finely cut noses with the form of forehead described above shows that there is considerable foreign blood in the Bergdama. Although they speak Hottentot, there is evidence that their language contains a number of words derived from various 'Sudanic' tongues. We may infer then that these people represent an old Negro stock which, though stated to have been carried into South-West Africa in the trail of the Hottentots, or perhaps even in part enslaved by them, is more likely to have been there before them. At the present day there are groups living in fixed villages and possessing goats, other groups living like Bushmen on the spoils of the chase and the fruits of the veld. A settlement usually consists of a small number of houses, perhaps not more than ten, each resembling a moderate-sized haystack in a European meadow. On the eastern side is the house of the 'great wife', i.e. the first wife of the village elder. All the houses face towards a tree in the centre of the village, and not far from this, in front of the house of the 'great wife', is the holy fire at which the elders sit and cook those portions of the meat of the bigger game to which they alone are entitled; here too they sit in council, no young man being allowed to approach until he has thrice proved himself a capable hunter at intervals of a year's time. If bad luck in hunting is persistent, or little *veldkos* is found, the suspicion will arise that someone has desecrated the holy fire. In spite of the importance of this fire it is uncertain whether the custom is originally of the Bergdama or has been taken over from the Herero.

5
Hamites (Eastern Hamites)

APART FROM RELATIVELY LATE SEMITIC INFLUENCE—whether
Phoenician (Carthaginian) and strictly limited, or Arab (Muhammadan) and widely diffused—the civilizations of Africa are the
civilizations of the Hamites, its history the record of these peoples
and of their interaction with the two other African stocks, the
Negro and the Bushman, whether this influence was exerted by
highly civilized Egyptians or by such wider pastoralists as are
represented at the present day by the Beja and the Somali.

To emphasize the importance of the Hamites and the part they
have played in Africa it is only necessary to refer to the map (Fig. 1)
which shows the distribution of languages in Africa at the present
day. It will be seen that Hamitic languages are spoken by peoples
spread over perhaps one-fifth of Africa, and Bernhard Struck
has been able to classify them into forty-seven stock languages
and seventy-one dialects. The area inhabited by people regarded
as Hamitic is even larger, including as it does many tribes
superficially semiticized under the influence of Islam, for
before the Arab expansion Hamitic languages must have been
spoken over by far the greater part of the northern half of the
continent.

The Hamites—who are 'Europeans', i.e. belong to the same
great branch of mankind as the whites—are commonly divided
into two great branches, Eastern and Northern.

(1) The Eastern Hamites comprise the ancient and modern
Egyptians (in the latter case recognizing the infusion of foreign
blood in the upper classes), the Beja, the Berberines (Barabra or

Nubians), the Galla, the Somali, the Danakil, and (though mixed with Semites and Negroes) most Ethiopians.

(2) The Northern Hamites include the Berbers of Cyrenaica, Tripolitania, Tunisia, and Algeria (often conventionally distinguished as Libyans), the Berbers of Morocco, the Tuareg and Tibu of the Sahara, the Fulbe of the Western Sudan, and the extinct Guanche of the Canary Islands.

Giuseppe Sergi points out that within such wideflung groups there is naturally much variation. Among the Eastern Hamites especially, the cranial characters though variable are, generally speaking, convergent, and are to be regarded as old variations of an original stock. To a great extent this is equally true of the face, which apart from Negro admixture is never prognathous; the nose is usually straight but sometimes aquiline, the lips are often thick, but never everted as in the Negro, the hair is often spiralled, but sometimes wavy or almost straight, the beard generally thin; the colour of the skin varies: it may be yellowish, coppery, red-brown, through every grade of *café-au-lait* to black, according to the amount of miscegenation that has taken place. Both divisions of the Hamites, according to Sergi, agree substantially in their bony structure, and thus form a single anthropological group, with skulls showing a considerable range of variation but constant in that each of the varieties he recognizes (Sergi has a special terminology for skulls) recurs in each great division, as in the main do the facial characteristics.

It is possible that some of these statements may require modification in the case of the Northern branch as it exists at the present day, since distinct foreign strains can be traced.

The Hamitic cradle-land is generally agreed to be Asiatic—perhaps Southern Arabia or possibly an area farther east, though Sergi and others suggest the Horn of Africa. Be this as it may, there is no doubt that the Hamites and Semites must be regarded as modifications of an original stock, and that their differentiation did not take place so very long ago, evidence for this statement being furnished by the persistence of common cultural traits and linguistic affinities. Physically their relationship is obvious, as also their kinship with the European representatives of the Mediterranean race, though some anthropologists admit this relationship only for the Northern branch of the Hamites, proposing to distinguish these from the Eastern branch by the term Libyan and calling the members of the Eastern branch Erythriotes.

We may begin our survey of the Hamites with the Eastern group, and this is the more convenient since apart from a few skeletal remains referred to the Old Stone Age—with which in this volume we are not concerned—the oldest 'Africans' of whom we have any organized knowledge belong to this group. These are the Egyptians of the predynastic period (anterior to about 3200 B.C.), best known as the proto-Egyptians. Both the high antiquity of the graves of the proto-Egyptians and the excellent condition of their contents make it convenient to begin our description of Hamitic Africa with some account of the racial history of Egypt, afterwards passing to the present-day representatives of the proto-Egyptian stock. The racial history of Egypt to the end of the Roman period has been summarized by Batrawi, from whom the following account is taken:

Since early neolithic times there existed two distinct but closely related types, a northern in Middle Egypt and a southern in Upper Egypt. The southern Egyptians were distinguished from the northerners by a smaller cranial index, a larger nasal index and greater prognathism. The geographical distinction between the two groups continued during the Pre-Dynastic period. The Upper Egyptians, however, spread into lower Nubia during that period. By the beginning of the Dynastic era the northern Egyptian type is encountered for the first time in the Thebaïd, i.e. in the southern territory. The incursion, however, seems to have been transitory and the effects of the co-existence of the two types in one locality remained very transient till the 18th Dynasty. From this time onwards the northern type prevailed all over Egypt, as far south as Denderah, till the end of the Roman period.

The predynastic Egyptian was of medium height, about 66 inches in the flesh, and dolichocephalic, with an index as regards the Naqada crania of some 73 (corresponding to about 75 in the living), both characters which, as we shall immediately see, are characteristic of a group of people known as Beja, who inhabit the Eastern Desert of Egypt, the Kassala Province of Sudan, and

extend through the former Italian colony of Eritrea into Ethiopia.
We shall return to this matter later, meanwhile describing something of the burial customs of the predynastic Egyptians.

The body usually lay upon the left side, with the arms and legs
flexed, in a shallow pit of oval or rectangular form at from two to
four feet below the surface. The direction of the long axis of the
graves is inconstant, but they are generally more or less parallel
to the local course of the river, the head of the deceased being
usually directed to the south. The grave was often lined with
matting and the body was sometimes wrapped in goat-skins or
linen, and lay surrounded by those valuable possessions which
the soul might be thought to require in the other world. These
objects included vessels of pottery and even of the hardest stone
—the latter worked with a skill which has seldom been attained
in any other place or time in the world's history—slate palettes,
beads, figurines, knives, and other implements, and occasionally
throwing-sticks and objects made of or covered with gold, while
copper occurs at first sporadically and then more commonly
throughout the whole predynastic period.

The Beja are divisible into four groups, which from north to
south are: (1) The Ababda of the Eastern Desert of Egypt; (2) the
Bisharin, also of the Egyptian desert, but extending some eighty
miles south of the Egypt-Sudan border and occupying a strip of
territory on the Atbara River; (3) the Hadendoa group, consisting
of a number of cognate tribes, of which the Hadendoa is the
strongest and best known; this group includes the Amarar, the
Nurab, the Ashraf, and the Artega, and extends as far south as
Tokar and the Khor Baraka; (4) the Beni Amer, occupying the
country to the south of the Khor Baraka, extending into Eritrea,
and even further into Ethiopia, where the type is found though
called by other names.

The Ababda, who once spoke To Bedawi, the language
(Hamitic) of the Bisharin and the Hadendoa, have lost their old
tongue and now speak Arabic; the Beni Amer speak both Bedawi
and the Semitic Tigrinya. Yet in spite of differences in language
the habits of the Beni Amer and Hadendoa are very similar,
although the latter—the 'Fuzzy Wuzzy' of the British soldier—
are on the whole a fiercer, wilder people; the Beni Amer—who

took no part in the fighting round El Teb during the Mahdia—
have presumably been softened in manner and habit by the same
Semitic cultural influence that has given them a Semitic language.
The Ababda to the north have to a considerable extent become
egyptianized, but the hills between the Nile and the Red Sea still
harbour a fair number of this people who adhere to their old
customs and lead very much their old style of life. The following
table shows the stature and cephalic index of these closely allied
tribes, together with the estimated stature of the predynastic
Egyptians from Naqada.

It will be realized that in the measurements given in the table
the cranial index of the proto-Egyptians has been increased by
two units to make it comparable with those of the Beni Amer
taken on the living subject.

	Stature	C.I.
Ababda	64 in.	73·7
Bisharin (Riverain) . . .	66 in.	78·4
Bisharin (Hill)	66½ in.	74·7
Hadendoa	65¾ in.	76·3
Beni Amer	64½ in.	74·7
Proto-Egyptians (Naqada) .	64 in.	74·9

As already mentioned (p. 64), the proto-Egyptians buried their
dead surrounded by all manner of necessities and luxuries, and
it is this habit that has enabled us to reconstruct so much of the
civilization of these early inhabitants of the Nile Valley. They
were agriculturists, growing crops of grain, but they also kept
goats and, towards the end of the period, as it would appear,
donkeys. They were keen hunters and fishermen, and a number of
copper harpoon-heads found, of the same pattern as the iron
weapons at present in use on the Upper Nile, show that they were
accustomed to hunting the hippopotamus. Added to this they
were admirable potters, and in the latter part of the predynastic
period attained the greatest skill in working hard stone into
beautifully shaped and proportioned vases. If we contrast this
civilization with that of their modern representatives, the Beja,
we find no close resemblances. The Beja by the nature of the
country they inhabit are nomad or semi-nomad pastoralists; the

camel, which they have probably possessed only for some 2,000 years, has given them a greater command over desert life than their early forebears can ever have had, and they thus occupy parts of the desert which in early days, if as we believe the climate was much the same as at present, must have been uninhabitable. It would then be surprising if they had developed the arts and crafts of the proto-Egyptians of the Nile Valley. There is, however, one interesting point of contact: the Bisharin still make stone pots, though for this purpose they use the softest stone obtainable, soap-stone so soft that it can be worked with a knife.

The social organization of the Beja is particularly interesting, because although they now include perhaps the most fanatical Muhammadans in East Africa, the majority, if not all, were heathen as recently as the life-time of the historian Makrizi (1366–1442), who wrote of them in the following terms:

They are nomads living in skin tents which they carry wherever they find grazing. Their genealogies are counted in the female line. Each tribe has a chief but they recognize no paramount. They have no religion. Property passes to the sons of sister and daughter to the prejudice of the sons of the deceased. To justify this custom they say that there can be no doubt as to the parentage of the son and daughter of a sister and these must belong to the family, whether their mother had gotten them by her husband or by another man. They formerly had a paramount chief to whom all the other chiefs were subordinate.

Makrizi adds that the Beja had many dromedaries and camels, besides sheep and cattle innumerable which provided them with meat and milk; in another passage he speaks of them as a people utterly irreligious and unintelligent, both men and women going naked and having no other covering than a loin-cloth, while the majority of them lacked even this.

Here is a perfectly definite account of a pagan, nomad, pastoral people, with matrilineal descent, living almost entirely upon the milk and flesh of their flocks. With the exception only of matrilineal descent—which has been given up owing to the introduction of Islam—and the wearing of Arab clothing, the picture drawn by Makrizi is that seen by any traveller in the remoter parts of the Eastern Desert at the present day. Moreover, a slight acquaintance with the people is enough to show that they retain indisputable traces of a former matriarchy. Their social organization even now is an extraordinarily interesting example of the persistence of older usages that are not contrary to the written word of the Koran. Thus, although descent is patrilineal as commanded by the Koran, among the Hadendoa a man goes to his bride's village to be married and stays there from one to three years, and almost the whole of the marriage-tent, and especially the marriage-bed, is provided by the bride's relatives; moreover the bridegroom has to do service to his father-in-law, helping him in all matters as a son, while in some communities there is a strict rule that the first child should be born among its mother's people.

As already stated, the Beja are essentially pastoralists, and on account of their love of their cattle show a special regard for milk, which is one of their most interesting characteristics and which on analysis can be shown to go back to an old Hamito-Semitic civilization. Even at the present day none of the Beha tribes milk into clay vessels or will put milk into them, in spite of the fact that many of them make good pots, nor would it be permissible to milk into the tin vessels introduced by European trade. Gourds and basketry vessels—the latter so well made as to hold milk without any tendency to leak—are considered the appropriate receptacles. Nor may a man drink the milk which he has himself drawn until someone else has taken a few sips; indeed, it would be a sore term of reproach to say of a man: 'He milked, and immediately drank.' There are also curious customs and prohibitions on the cooking of milk. Especially do the Beja despise, for example, some of the Arab tribes for allowing their women to milk their animals. All these facts indicate that milk is not 'common', using the word in the Biblical sense. It might indeed almost be called sacred or sacrosanct, and as noted in Chapter 7 this holds equally for such tribes as the Masai and Nandi of East Africa, who have much Hamitic blood in their veins.

To return to the Nile Valley proper. In Egypt there is evidence of a gradual modification in the population from the beginning of dynastic times, so that by the Pyramid period the population of Egypt was of a heavier build, with a broader skull and face and a heavier jaw, the roundness of skull being determined by an increase of breadth rather than by general increase in the dimensions of the skull. These are the people portrayed in such magnificent works of art of the Pyramid period as the 'Scribes' of Giza and the Louvre, and the Sheikh el Beled, and they no doubt represent the type of a considerable part of the population of the Ancient Kingdom. Culturally they were the creators of the finest statuary, wall paintings, and sculptures in low relief to which Egypt attained, and it was their work that the consciously archaistic Egyptians of the Twenty-sixth Dynasty endeavoured to imitate as representing the highest development of their national art. But what has been written applies only to the natives of Upper and Middle Egypt. We have no knowledge of what was happening in the Delta through dynastic and predynastic times; the remains, if any persist, are hidden under great masses of alluvial deposits.

The type described persisted and probably increased in number through dynastic times, and it is in fact that of the fellahin of the present day. The modern Egyptian, with a stature of about 66 inches, shows no great variation as between different parts of Egypt. He is persistently long-headed, with a cephalic index varying round about 75. However, in passing southwards there is a slight tendency towards negritization: it has been pointed out that the eye and skin colour darken, that the proportion of unusually broad noses increases, and that spiral and crisp hair becomes more frequent.

Foreigners often profess to be able to distinguish at sight between Muslims and Copts, but since physical analysis indicates no substantial difference the distinction, if it exists, must be essentially cultural, due to habits and traits dependent on mode of life. The Copts—Christians, and predominantly town-dwellers —are particularly clerks and shopkeepers, while the great majority of fellahin are peasants. Perhaps then the effect of respectively subservient and dominant habits has brought about a perceptible difference; it is true that slight differences in the character of the face have been described, the Copts having lighter eyes and skin colour and a slightly thinner nose, but in spite of this it may be doubted whether the diagnosis at sight between Copt and Muslim is not wholly a matter of such factors as gait and dress.

It is perhaps worth while to draw attention here to the existence among the present population of ancient folk beliefs and customs. There is in existence a papyrus—dating from the time of Rameses II, or possibly his successor—which not only marks lucky and unlucky days but gives instructions as to how their unfortunate character may be averted. The five epagomenal days of the old Egyptian calendar were regarded as unlucky, the instructions being: 'Do not do any work on these things: wheat, spelt, flax, clothing. Do not devise anything at all;' and in modern Egypt we find it said that a child begotten during the epagomenal days will be misshapen, this also applying to animals, so that cattle and mares are not covered during this period; there is a general, though perhaps less intense, belief that neither sowing nor planting should be undertaken. An even more striking example is presented by a day near the end of the month of Choiak. The papyrus marks the 26th of this month as most unlucky, the warning being, 'Do not eat fish; those living in the midst of Tattu turn themselves into the fish An.' The last sentence contains a mythological reference that we cannot appreciate, but in the modern calendar the note for the 11th of Muharram, which corresponds to the old 26th of Choiak, is this: 'The eating of pigeons is liked, that of fish disliked.' It is not suggested that these instances are actually older than some of the folk beliefs of our own and other European countries; their great interest seems to be that the date at which they were written down, not necessarily for the first time, is known, and conclusively demonstrates how a lucky or unlucky day may persist through a change of calendar, being transferred to the new calendar and accepted by the adherents of a religion, commonly regarded as fanatical, whose leaders would undoubtedly brand the belief as highly superstitious and unorthodox.

South of Egypt proper lies Nubia, with a political boundary at Wadi Halfa between Egypt and the Sudan. This arrangement is entirely artificial, for racially (as geographically) the transition takes place at the First Cataract. Nevertheless, lower Nubia was in earlier days so dominated by Egypt that in the year 1879 B.C.

the Pharaoh decreed that the Second Cataract should be the northern limit of Negroland, which no Negro should pass except on a definite mission or when coming to trade for a limited period. The stele at Semma near the cataract reads:

Southern boundary, made in the year 8, under the majesty of the King of Upper and Lower Egypt, Khekure [Sesostris III] who is given life for ever and ever; in order to prevent that any Negro should cross it, by water or by land, with a ship [or] any herds of the Negroes; except a Negro who shall come to do trading in Iken or with a commission. Every good thing shall be done with them, but without allowing a ship of the Negroes to pass by Heh, going downstream, for ever.

Immediately above the First Cataract the traveller is struck by a new language, generally admitted to belong to the great (Negro) Sudanic family, though one authority has regarded it as basically Hamitic but heavily negritized. Be this as it may, the Nubians themselves—commonly known as Barabra, though calling themselves Nubi—must be regarded as predominantly Hamitic. Tall, and mainly long-headed, those belonging to the less negritized type are of a slight, rather graceful build, which immediately distinguishes them from the fellahin. They are darker-skinned and narrower-faced, however, and though the hair is frequently curly it is seldom as crisp as that of a Negro, the occurrence of individuals reproducing the head-shape of the proto-Egyptian type being not very uncommon. How this comes about will be best understood by considering their history. The skeletal remains recovered from excavations during Archaeological Surveys undertaken by the Egyptian Government on two different occasions prior to the raising of the Aswan Dam show that some 3,000 years B.C. Nubia was inhabited by a people similar to the predynastic Egyptians, with a civilization essentially resembling that of the latter, if rather less advanced. As might be expected this people traded freely with the Egyptians, as is clear by the discovery in their graves of typical late predynastic Egyptian objects of the finest type, including, e.g. a magnificent gold-handled stone mace. Naturally the connexion did not end at this remote period: the history of Nubia, known with fair accuracy from Egyptian sources, shows Egypt in a condition of continual trade and intermittent warfare with the peoples south of the

First Cataract, from the time of the Pyramid-builders until, under the New Empire, Nubia was thoroughly egyptianized. During all this time, and indeed much later, we can trace the gradual ebb and flow of influence from the north, according to the condition of Egypt at the time. After the Pyramid period Nubia must have sunk back during the dark period from the Sixth to the Eleventh Dynasty; she emerges into the light again in the Twelfth Dynasty, and a repetition of this to-and-fro movement no doubt took place during the periodic fluctuations of Egyptian influence south of the cataract. There is also evidence of considerable pressure by the Beja peoples of the Eastern Desert. Hence there arose in Nubia a hybrid population, blending the characters of Egyptian, Negro, and Beja, and it is this type —which can clearly be defined in the graves of the Middle Empire (i.e. the Twelfth to the Seventeenth Dynasty)—that has in the main persisted in Nubia to the present day, allowance being made for a new incoming round-headed influence which certainly existed in this part of the country about the beginning of the Christian era and which may have been reinforced indirectly by the Arab invasions (discussed in Chapter 10).

The Barabra of the present day are usually recognized as belonging to four main divisions, which may well be called tribes, and, although they have adopted the Arabs' social organization, the names of a number of their tribal sections point back to the Beja element in their origin. The following are the tribal units generally recognized: the Kenuz, of the country in the neighbourhood of the Wadi Kenuz and between Aswan and Korosko, who consider themselves descendants of the Arabic Beni Kenz; the Feyadicha, extending southwards to Wadi Halfa; the Mahas, from Wadi Halfa to Dongola; the Danagla, in the neighbourhood of Dongola.

The Barabra are an enterprising people, travellers and traders, not unscholarly, and quick at picking up languages, so that they are found everywhere as settlers between the Delta and Khartoum, the qualities which fit them for adventures in foreign parts being especially marked in the Danagla, who have appreciably influenced the culture of northern Kordofan and formed a considerable part of the personnel of the Arab slave-raiders of the middle of the last century. The poorness of their country is no doubt largely responsible for their dispersion, for, though they are an agricultural people wherever this is possible, over a great part of their territory the desert closes in to within a few yards of the river.

The Barabra scar their cheeks with vertical or oblique cuts on each side of the face, and they mutilate their girls in the same way as do the Arab tribes of the south. Although the women now wear the Arab robe it is scarcely more than eighty years since their customary garment was a short petticoat reaching to the knees. Their hand-made pottery is particularly good; they make excellent baskets and mats, and Burchhardt mentions having frequently seen small looms in their houses.

The country between the frontiers of Sudan and Kenya and the sea, though composed of three political units (from north to south—Ethiopia, French Somaliland, and Somalia), possesses such fundamental racial unity that its peoples cannot well be described separately. Everywhere in this area the population is Hamitic, or has at least an Hamitic basis, the only exception being the Shankalla, the Negro or heavily negritized tribes occupying the western and southern slopes of the Ethiopian tableland. Some of these have been mentioned (p. 55); here it is only necessary to state that this term is not tribal but merely the Amharic for 'Negro', and so is applied by the Ethiopians to all tribes with noticeable Negroid characters.

Racially the former Italian colony of Eritrea differs little from the neighbouring portion of the Kassala Province of the Sudan, though there are a few scattered Negro enclaves near Barentu (e.g. the Barea and Kunama). In the north-west are the Beni Amer near Keren are the Bogos (now Roman Catholic), who speak a Cushitic language (termed Bilen), as do the Saho round Annesley Bay south of Massawa.

In Ethiopia proper the aboriginal population is generally assumed to have been Negro. If this be true it is possible that their remains are to be seen in some of the lowly Negroid hunting peoples scattered over much of Ethiopia, such as those known to the Galla and Ethiopians as Wata, and to the Kafficho as Manjo.

Be this as it may, there seems no reason to doubt that the Hamites were entering the country at irregular intervals over a prolonged period and were in East Africa some thousands of years B.C., with the result that the present inhabitants of Ethiopia are broadly a mixture of Hamite and Negro, carrying perhaps 80 per cent. of Hamitic blood, with a leavening of Semites whose influence—since physically they resemble the Hamites—can be traced only by cultural and historical criteria. The Semitic languages, Ge'ez and Amharic, may be assumed to mark out the area most affected by their immigrations, it being always remembered that there is a dual tendency over the whole of this area to exaggerate the Semitic element—by the Ethiopians on the one hand on account of their old Jewish connexion and the traditional descent of their royal family from the Queen of Sheba, and by the Somali and cognate peoples owing to their desire to accentuate the historical implications of the religion they have adopted. The term Cushite is often applied to that section of the Hamites found in Ethiopia (linguistically Cushite and Cushitic definitely have this sense), so that the Ethiopians proper might be described as semiticized Cushites, in opposition to the purer Cushites of the north (Bogos, etc.), the centre (Agau), and the south (Kafficho, Walamo, etc.).

As might be inferred from what has already been said, the inhabitants of northern Ethiopia exhibit a relationship to the Beja, but are much more mixed: thus, while the Emperor Haile Selassie might almost pass for a south European, his predecessor was in feature distinctly negroid. Apart from negroid characters the skulls of northern Ethiopians are of the proto-Egyptian type, though a certain number are higher and rounder; indeed a group of ninety-four skulls contained 5 per cent. of brachycephals while none occurred in two series of over fifty each of Beni Amer and Hadendoa. Some such result as this might be expected in view of the historical connexion of Ethiopia with Arabia, and it is supported by Schweinfurth's account of the northern Ethiopians. He describes them as 'a very mixed race', and goes on to say that although he

paid attention to thousands . . . [he] always failed to find a single common feature, a characteristic peculiarity in their appearance, by which, in the majority of cases, they might be distinguished from the other ... races of this district, for instance, the Hamitic ... Habab, and Beni Amer. The one thing ... binding them together is their speech, a branch of the old Ge'ez. ...

Turning then to linguistics, we find that the languages spoken in Ethiopia are not only of great interest in themselves but are important as being, so far as we know, the oldest Semitic languages spoken in Africa. The Ethiopians have been Christians since the fourth century, and the Bible was translated into Ethiopic, or Ge'ez—a language akin to both Hebrew and Arabic, but closer to an ancient tongue of southern Arabia known as Sabaean—by the seventh century. In the thirteenth century a particular dialect known as Amharic became the official language of the court and government, the province of Amhara having obtained a predominance which it maintained until the nineteenth century. This language, which is still written in Ethiopic, has diverged greatly from the ancient Semitic type, so that some have called it Hamitic rather than Semitic. The more modern representative of Ethiopic, and one undoubtedly Semitic, is the Tigrinya spoken in the northern provinces of Ethiopia, including Eritrea, and in the extreme south-east of the Kassala Province of the Sudan.

Of the older Cushitic languages a certain number are important because they are spoken by influential peoples: such are the Somali and Galla in the south, the Afar (sometimes called Danakil) in the east, the Agau in the centre, and the Bogos (also known as Bilin), of Agau origin, in the north.

Ethiopia is not only a country of racial confusion, but also of religious confusion, for here are found pagans (many Galla), Muhammadans (many Galla and Somali in the south, Beni Amer, Saho, etc., in the north), Christians and even Jews; the last the Falasha, the so-called 'black' Jews of Ethiopia. As regards all these confessions: Ethiopian Islam, though Sunnite, is little orthodox, there exist no theological schools connected with mosques, nor are there any of those religious brotherhoods which have done so much for Islam in North Africa; hence indifference to and imperfect knowledge of the observances of Islam, and even the presence at Christian ceremonies of such people as the Beni Amer. Christianity probably reached Ethiopia from Syria; the King of 'Semitic' Aksum was converted about A.D. 350, and somewhat later came a dark period in Ethiopian history during which time the great saints of the Ethiopian Church performed so many miracles. It must have been during this period that Ethiopia sought contact with the Egyptian Church, with the result that Ethiopian Christianity is Coptic (monophysite), receives its patriarch (*abuna*) from Alexandria, and still preserves in its church services the use of the old Egyptian sistrum, long disused in its country of origin.

A good deal of interest has been taken in the 'black' Jews, the Falasha (from the Ethiopic *falas*, 'stranger'), though little is known about them. Tradition states that the Queen of Sheba, who was a princess of Aksum, was instructed in the Jewish religion when she visited Solomon, and on her return introduced it into her own country. This is, of course, legendary, but there does seem to have been some unrecorded connexion between Judaism and Ethiopia—perhaps before the introduction of Christianity—for there are a number of Old Testament practices in Ethiopian Christianity. Moreover, the Aramaic loan-words denoting religious ideas in the older Ethiopian texts are of Jewish-Aramaean rather than Christian-Aramaean origin: e.g. those connected with the observance of the Sabbath, which has even been personified as a female saint; the distinction between clean and unclean animals; and ideas of ritual uncleanliness. Therefore, since there is no record of the conversion of the Falasha, it has been suggested that their Jewish faith is a survival of the early connexion alluded to above.

The Falasha live for the most part in villages of their own, and until 1800, when they became subject to the Ethiopian kingdom of Tigré, had their own 'kings', claiming descent from David. An industrious people, skilled in agriculture and in the manufacture of pottery, ironware, and cloth, and good masons, they hold themselves aloof from the other peoples of the land and generally have a higher standard of morals than their neighbours. They do not practise polygamy, and never marry out of their own people. Entering a Christian house is strictly forbidden; if this is done, ritual purification is necessary. They are divided into three sects, each with its high priest, and they fast twice a week and for forty days before Easter. Their ritual contains various pagan elements:

D

as already stated the Sabbath has been deified and, as the Goddess Sanbat, receives adoration and sacrifices; a woman guilty of unchastity has to be purified by leaping through flames; no newly built house is considered habitable until the blood of a sheep or a fowl has been spilt on it. Celibacy is not practised by the priests, though they may not marry a second time; there is a monastic system, introduced it is said in the fourth century A.D. The numbers of the Falasha are estimated by Cerulli at about 30,000.

The Galla (calling themselves Ilm Orma, and often known as Oromo), perhaps the most interesting people in Ethiopia, appear in history in the sixteenth century, when they invaded southern Ethiopia from the west, at a time when the invasion of Muhammad Granye was distracting the attentions of the Ethiopians elsewhere; they were thus able to establish themselves there unopposed. Apart from colour—which varies greatly, some Borana being lighter than 'brown' and the Wallage and Itu much darker —the Galla are described as remarkably uniform in physical type. They are tall ($67\frac{1}{2}$ inches), dolichocephals (C.I. 76), and have a high and broad forehead and regular features. The majority are still pagan, though definitely Muhammadan and Christian groups also exist. Although living nominally under Ethiopian institutions, and providing the bulk of the cavalry of the Ethiopian army, the Galla formerly had a highly complex system of social organization which to some extent still persists. Under this the people were divided into groups, called *gada*, arranged in pairs, each man entering the group of his grandfather. Each pair of groups passed through five successive period of eight years each. The men of the fourth period were responsible for and ruled the country, the Abba Boku (father of the sceptre) being elected from this group.

With the exception of the Borana nomads the Galla are now mainly an agricultural people, but cattle are still the most valued form of wealth, and the attainment of 1,000 head of stock is marked by a special ceremony. The agricultural Galla use a primitive plough drawn by camels or oxen.

While it is at present impossible to say what relation Galla religion bears to that of their forebears of pre-Christian and pre-Muhammadan times, the fact that they constitute the only surviving group of any size of pagan Hamites makes their religious ideas of the highest interest. They recognize a supreme deity, Wak or Waka (heaven, sky), and a subordinate god and goddess, Oglie and Atete, while at every new moon the head of the household (who acts as priest at all religious functions) sacrifices to the unseen moon, adjuring her to ask the coming new moon to continue to protect his cattle, etc. Certain animals are said to be sacred, including the snake, the crocodile, and the owl (there is, however, no evidence that these are totems), and, at least among the southern Galla, there is a well-defined tree cult: great reverence is paid to the baobab, milk being poured over its roots once a month, while once a year 'they kill for it a black sheep'; they also honour a number of other trees, e.g. the wild fig, and one called *karayu*, which is also the name of a clan who will not cut down this tree. Divination is performed by inspection of the stomach of a slaughtered cow, and interpretation of the flight of birds. The chief religious act is the *wadaja*, or offering of common prayer; the ceremony is accompanied by a sacrificial meal, a portion of which is offered to Wak. Until prohibited by the Ethiopians, an important feature of the Galla religion was the pilgrimage to Wallage to the Abba Muda ('father of unction'), the supreme religious authority of the people, said to live in a mysterious cave with a serpent. The pilgrims were catechized on the law of Wak and the customs of the Galla and exhorted against Islam, the Abba Muda anointing their heads with butter. Only men might take part, and every family was expected to send a representative at least once in three generations.

The Galla wear a petticoat or tunic and the *tobe* (cotton sheet), with sometimes a sheep- or leopard-skin over their shoulders; some women combine a cotton wrap with a skin undergarment. In war they carry two light javelins, a heavy spear, and a small round shield. Their huts are circular, with vertical walls of clay or rough stone and conical thatched roofs. Cotton-weaving was formerly a notable industry, and good metal and leather work was produced; among many Galla the smiths form a distinct caste.

Monogamy is general, except among the Borana, and the bride-price is paid in cattle. A widow is inherited by her husband's brother, together with any children she has borne. The family is patriarchal, the father having the power of life and death over his children, whom he may even sell into slavery. The eldest son is the chief heir; women have no right of inheritance. Unchastity in women before marriage is extremely rare, and legally disqualifies them for wedlock.

The early history of the Somali is obscure; that they are essentially Hamitic is certain. Physically they are not unlike the Galla, of the same average stature ($67\frac{1}{2}$ inches) but with a lower cephalic index (about 74). Their colour varies from light to dark brown, or even darker, 'black' skins being common enough in the East African ports in individuals calling themselves Somali. As is usual among nomadic desert men compelled to lead an abstemious life, they are very enduring under hardship, and can subsist for a considerable time upon a minimum of food and water. Observers lay stress on their cheerful, light-hearted character, as well as upon their inordinate conceit and their insatiable avarice; it is perhaps because of these qualities that, when well led, the Somali has proved a reliable soldier, but though generally easy-going he can, on occasion, develop a rather surprising religious fanaticism, as shown by the episode of the 'Mad' Mullah as well as in recurring periods of unrest under other less gifted leaders. Each tribe has a chief, chieftainship being confined to a single family, but, as usual among nomads, the power of the chief is generally small, and the office entails at least as many troublesome duties as privileges.

According to the Somali their nation is composed of two main groups, the Somali and the Sab; the latter include the two group-ings known as Digil and Rahanwein, while the Dir, Hawiya, Gadabursi, and Darod are classed as Somali. Elaborate genealo-gies are produced to support these statements, but there is no obvious difference in physical type; if there originally was any it has long ago been lost.

The Afar, or Danakil, who speak a language akin to the Somali, inhabit a roughly triangular area north of the Somali and Galla, bounded on the east by the sea and on the west by the eastern scarp of the Ethiopian plateau. They are described as particularly thin men, with an average height of about 66 inches, with features 'of Semitic type, regular and handsome'. Their skin is said to be as dark as that of many Negroes, their hair coarse and curly but not spiralled. There is a dominant class, or nobility, distinguished as Asaimara or 'red men', in contradistinction to the Adoimara or 'white men', the two classes standing in the relationship of conquerors and conquered, though there is no difference in colour at the present day—indeed, it seems doubtful if there ever was. Rather is the difference one dependent on the invasion of the land by a people not essentially different from the early occupants expanding towards the coast from the Ethiopian plateau. The Danakil profess Islam, but their practice is lax, and they lack regular priests or teachers.

Geographical position suggests the mention in this chapter of the outcast, or more picturesquely 'pariah', tribes of Eastern Africa and Ethiopia, though the term seems overstrong for such peoples as the Midgan (hunters, sweepers, and surgeons), Tomal (smiths), and Yibir (leather-workers) of the Somali, all grouped together under the heading Sāb. It has been assumed that the area was formerly peopled by Negrillos, and that the outcasts are their descendants. However, it is noteworthy that such peoples as the Dorobo (Okiek) of Kenya—symbiotes, if the term be permitted, of such strong pastoralists as the Masai and Nandi—do not present any suggestion of a pygmy ancestry: they are in fact well-grown men and women, some obviously carrying so much Hamitic blood that they might be grouped with the Nilo-Hamites. This does not necessarily negative the idea of their being the remains of an earlier population, but it does seem to imply that any contact with pygmy tribes was but slight and perhaps not even at first hand, the 'older' element being not essentially pygmy but rather Negro, and their use of bow and poisoned arrow—the typical weapon of the pygmy peoples—being due to mediate rather than actual contact. Investigation of the 'submerged classes', the *dupi*, of the Bari of the extreme southern Sudan (p. 109) bears out this view. Many of these *dupi* are sturdy, broad-faced, broad-nosed blacks, as opposed to at least some of the narrower-faced 'commoners', the latter often men with higher bridges to their noses as well as less flaring nostrils.

The Dorobo are divided into three main groups in Kenya and Tanzania, those of Kenya being associated with forest. They are a purely hunting people, and all speak dialects of Nandi, but unlike the latter they possess no domesticated animals except the dog; they carry spears as well as arrows, and make great use of game pits, while some communities have weighted drop-spears for rhinoceros and elephant.

The Wata, to give them their Galla name, constitute scattered, little-known groups in southern Ethiopia.

6
Hamites (Northern Hamites)

BEFORE DESCRIBING THE PEOPLES included in this vast group (and how vast it is will best be realized by looking at the map on p. 6, and neglecting all indications of Arabic influence west of the Nile) it must be emphasized that the northern states constituting its political units—Libya, Tunisia, Algeria, and Morocco—are from the anthropological standpoint entirely artificial, their boundaries in no instance coinciding with any geographical or racial division. It is also essential to realize that the number of Arabs entering North Africa was never very great, and that the social results of intermarriage and the prestige of the dominant religion account for the arabization—so far as it has taken place— of Tunisia and Algeria far more than a substitution of Arab for Berber blood. In Libya the matter stands rather differently: apart from the narrow littoral belt, which intercepts the greater part of the rainfall, the climatological conditions are such that the country (whatever may have been the case in Roman times) consists almost entirely of desert or poor steppe, apt enough for nomads or semi-nomads but offering little attraction to sedentary cultivators. Thus it is that in Eastern Libya we have such true Arabs as the Aulad Ali described in Chapter 10. Neglecting these and their congeners we may begin our description of the Berbers by pointing out that excavations at Mersa Matruh, in the neighbourhood of the western Egyptian frontier, suggest that at a period perhaps as remote as the third millennium B.C. the population of the coastal plain had a culture similar to that of the proto-Egyptians, their well-made stone pots being highly significant in this respect, though they differ in shape and design from any found in the Nile Valley. Of a later date are the skeletons found at Roknia in Algeria, buried in true dolmens, i.e. in tombs consisting of entire single slabs and not of built-up courses of stone. Their data is uncertain; their latest limit certainly falls within the Iron Age, itself of indefinite date in North Africa, yet the skulls include examples of proto-Egyptian type, as well as heavier rounder skulls which can probably be related to the round-heads described on p. 83. Here, then, in the prehistoric period are present at least two of the types which, as we shall immediately see, can be recognized in the population of North Africa at the present day, but before referring to these in detail it will be well to say something about the blond Berbers, concerning the Nordic affinities of many of whom so much has been written.

It is first necessary to stress the white quality of the skin of the Berber tribes generally, and to realize that the skin, even where it it most exposed, 'burns to the tint peculiar to white men and resembles that of the fairer rather than of the darker races even among these'. The Shawia of the Aures Mountains of Algeria, among whom blonds are at least as frequent as elsewhere, are, 'generally speaking, remarkably European in their appearance', so that many might pass for Irishmen or Scotchmen.

The boys in particular when about the age of 15 or 16 would if put into similar dress be almost indistinguishable from English lads of the same age . . . [but] it would certainly occur to an observer that the preponderance of dark hair was in excess of what would be found in most English districts. Fair-haired men as blond even as North Germans are to be seen . . . but even taking a village by itself there was no instance in which their numbers seemed to equal those of the dark-haired men, ordinarily they were in a very small minority . . . on the other hand, it has hardly perhaps been sufficiently noticed that all without exception, whether their hair or eyes be dark or light, are invariably fair-skinned, much fairer than a typical Tuscan or Spaniard.

As against this statement Coon observes that although the Shawia approach the traditional conception of the Nordics in their light skin colour, stature, trunk, limb, and head measurements, 96 per cent. have black hair and only about 30 per cent. light or mixed eyes, and he does not believe that the anthropometric data

relating to them are adequate for any hard-and-fast pronounce-
ments on their 'Nordicity'. Later work on these people by
Kossovitch confirms such an opinion.

If the inhabitants of the Aures Mountains constitute a fair
sample, then in a general way the Berbers of Algeria may be
described as spare in build, averaging about 67 inches in stature,
with black hair and brown or hazel eyes. The women, who wither
early, are in other respects the smaller counterparts of the men,
their invariably dark hair being due to frequent dyeing with gall-
nut.

The light to medium brown-skinned, black-haired inhabitants of
the oases west of the Nile Valley and in the kingdom of Libya, e.g.
Kharga, Siwa, Aujila, and Magiabra, are as a rule extremely
dolichocephalic (C.I. for Siwa and Aujila 72), with heads low in
the crown, short, narrow faces, and mesorrhine noses. In general
their stature is short, about 64 inches. According to Coon, they
represent a distinct Mediterranean type of some antiquity. The
lighter-skinned, arabized Berber agriculturists of Cyrenaica
include several physical types, but dolichocephaly is universal
(C.I. 74–77) and average statures vary between 66 and 67½ inches.
Their relative tallness, narrow but not short faces, and leptor-
rhiny, distinguish them from the oasis-dwellers. Coon describes
one numerically important Cyrenaican type as representing the
'standard' Libyan of the Egyptian monuments, with a receding
forehead and a high skull-vault, no development of brow-ridges,
and a high-rooted convex nose. The North African Arabs from
Libya to Morocco, who are taller than most Berbers, have a
similar forehead, combined with a protruding occiput. The nose
is prominent and narrow. A few of those in the coastal regions of
Cyrenaica are brachycephalic.

Even apart from a considerable Jewish element of long standing in the cities, and recent European settlers, great racial complexity exists in Algeria and Tunisia. The oasis Berbers of
Ghardaya and Biskra resemble the people of the Egyptian and
Libyan oases in their shortness and pigmentation, but have
broader heads (C.I. 77) and a leptorrhine nasal index. The
Kabyles of the Tizi Ouzou region of Algeria are somewhat taller,

64¾ inches, have a similar value for the cephalic index and are also leptorrhine. These results are given by Coon and Briggs, who analysed and completed Kidder's observations (1927) on over 300 adult male Kabyles. According to them, the Kabyles, often described as one of the three principal groups of blond Berbers (the others being the Shawia described above and the Riffians of Morocco), are in fact no fairer than the most typical Mediterraneans. A flattening at the top of the occiput and the everted angles of the jaws seem to indicate a persistence of a physical type which, as Briggs has shown, formed the basis of the population of North Africa in Neolithic times, and a slight but perceptible frequency of spiralled hair suggests contacts with trans-Saharan Negroes or Negroids.

The Negroids found in various parts of the country west of Libya require no particular description. As might be expected, they are most numerous in the south. The type found in the Island of Jerba (Tunisia), which has its counterparts on the mainland opposite as well as along the littoral in the neighbourhood of Bu Ajilat, is of medium stature (65 inches) and sub-brachycephalic or brachycephalic (C.I. 81–82) with a relatively narrower face and a broader nose than most North Africans. The head is high in the crown, brow ridges are well developed, and there is some occipital flattening.

In Morocco about two-thirds of the people are Berber-speaking, compared with one-third in Algeria. The best-known Moroccan Berbers, the Riffian tribes, are also the most Nordic. Average heights for different tribes range from 65 to 68 inches, the mean for all being 66½. Head shape is invariably dolichocephalic (C.I. 75) and nasal form leptorrhine (N.I. 61–65), the value of the nasal index increasing from east to west. The Riffians have pinkish-white skins similar to those of northern Europeans in about 65 per cent. of the group as a whole, and the figure rises to 80 per cent. among the central tribes. Hair colour ranges from black to medium or dark brown in 90 per cent. of cases, the remainder being reddish or light brown and, in not quite 1 per cent., golden blond. Beards are less dark than head hair, and the face and body are as hirsute as in northern Europe. In only 2 per cent. are the eyes pure blue, 55 per cent. having otherwise light or mixed green-, grey-, or blue-brown, and 43 per cent. dark brown eyes. Coon remarks that the Rif is not a blond country in the sense that the Scandinavian peninsula or even England are blond, but is more so than the greater part of Spain or southern Italy.

These then, apart from the Arab element, constitute the racial types that it is possible to differentiate in the Berber population of western Libya, Tunisia, Algeria, and Morocco, and since each of these races has its known centre of origin—or at least of dispersion—it becomes possible to indicate the part played by various stocks in the history of North Africa. As might be expected, there is no difficulty in recognizing the dark, mesorrhine to leptorrhine long-heads of short to medium height as the North African representatives of the proto-Egyptian stock of the Nile Valley.

Though some would deny this, there is only one white stock from which the taller, narrow-nosed long-heads can be derived, namely the Nordic of Europe. Briefly, the measurements of Nordics in northern Europe give stature and cephalic, facial, and nasal indices so near to those of the taller Berbers that there can be no doubt that either the latter are derived from the former or they share a common origin. This identification makes clear the source of the blond, light-eyed Berbers described above, these being none other than individuals in whom the Nordic strain is strong enough to manifest itself in its traditional physical characters.

The date at which the Nordics entered North Africa is unknown, but that it is relatively remote is proved by the occurrence in an Egyptian tomb of the New Empire of a painting of light-skinned, green-eyed, fair-haired Libyans. Apart from the intrinsic interest of this painting it is of great archaeological importance as disposing finally of such ill-considered suggestions as that which makes the blond Berbers the descendants of the Vandal invaders of the fifth century.

The problem connected with the third group, the brachycephals or sub-brachycephals of medium stature, is less easy. The suggestion that they are the descendants of the shorter brachycephals of the coast of southern Arabia, though the obvious one to make, presents difficulties in view of the relatively wide dispersion of the type. It might fairly be argued that so large a proportion of the conquerors of Spain (who came from North Africa and were later driven back there) were of southern Arabian origin that this would explain the wide distribution of round-heads among the Berbers. Bertholon and Chantre, although they note that the skulls of the Berber brachycephals or sub-brachycephals are not globular as are those of the European round-heads (Alpine race) and that the occipital region is flattened and the cranial vault very high (i.e. in general appearance these skulls resemble the round-headed population of Asia Minor rather than Europe), yet seem to consider that many of the short brachycephals of North Africa are more closely related to the brachycephals of France (Alpine race) than to those of Asia Minor. In endeavouring to come to a conclusion it must not be assumed that the same influence has been exerted equally, alike inland in the hills and in the coastal zone. With regard to the latter the enormous influence from the end of the fifteenth century onward of the 'Barbary pirates', largely of Levantine origin, must not be forgotten; the North African coast was their home, and although they were occasionally defeated by the Christian medieval powers they were never broken. Moreover, Jerba, one of the centres of round-headedness, is known to have been one of their strongholds. It would seem fair, then, to regard the coastal round-heads as owing their existence largely to this Levantine influence, and this would account for the high skull with flattened occiput.

The extinct Guanches of the Canary Islands showed at least as much racial mixture as their brethren of the mainland. Their remains indicate that besides tall fair dolichocephalic and shorter dark mesocephalic elements, there was present a round-headed element, akin to the Alpines of Central Europe.

Most Berbers are pastoralists, and some are also skilled agriculturists and gardeners. Some of the pastoralists practise an elaborate form of transhumance (the periodic to-and-fro movement of herds between definite regions of varying climate) differing from the familiar lowland-to-mountain type of Mediterranean lands in that there is a double movement, summer and winter, the latter, in the Middle Atlas, taking the tribes hundreds of miles from 'home' so that they become virtually nomadic.

The social organization of the Berber differs entirely from that of the Arab, being as essentially democratic and suited to a sedentary life as that of the latter is aristocratic and apt for the nomadic existence. But although this typical contrast is true for by far the greater part of Barbary, it must be realized that it is not absolute. There are many sedentary Arabs in the country and some nomad Berbers; moreover, it is always difficult to decide whether any particular people not obviously Berber or Arab are to be regarded as arabized Berbers or as berberized Arabs. Some assistance in doubtful cases can be gained by considering their geographical position, the Arabs presenting a diminishing percentage of the population from east to west. Berbers in Tunisia are found in isolated masses, e.g. as a group of Abadite heretics on the Island of Jerba, and in the far south. Some of the purest Berber groups in Barbary inhabit the Kabyle hills and the Aures Mountains.

The following account, though referring specifically to the social organization of the Kabyle, may be taken as typical of the political and social organization of the Berbers as a whole (excepting the Tuareg), the essential feature of their society being the existence of a great number of small democratic communities, each entirely independent and governed solely by the will of the people.

The village is the administrative unit, to which the most complete autonomy is allowed. Two or more villages may be connected by administrative ties (not those of kinship) to form a tribe, and the union of several such tribes constitutes a confederation. In time of war only, a head is appointed for each tribe and for the confederation, but in ordinary times the confederation never interferes in the affairs of the tribe unless directly appealed to. The tribe takes no part in the local government of its villages, but performs certain administrative duties, e.g. the making of roads, the management of tribal property such as mosques, tombs of saints, and educational establishments, with the levying of the necessary taxes for these; it determines questions of war and peace, and acts as arbiter in disputes between villages. A general assembly of the tribe is practically unknown, and its affairs are ordinarily managed by a deputation of the chief men from each of its various villages. These delegates do not hold any permanent office, but each village can send an indefinite number.

The effective government of the village is vested in the *jemâa*, the general assembly of the citizens, of which every adult man is a member. It meets once a week, and in theory every member has a right to speak, though in practice this right is only exercised by the elders and heads of families. For important decisions unanimity is required, and if the assembly fails to agree, reference may be made to the *jemâa* of another village or to some individual arbiter. The powers of the *jemâa* cover every matter great or small which concerns the village; it exercises judicial authority both in civil and in criminal cases (the latter jurisdiction now curtailed by the State), and has the right to interfere in the private life of the individual.

The Amin (or Amekkeran), 'chief', is appointed by the *jemâa* to hold the reins of government and carry out its decisions. As he constitutes the sole executive of the village state his duties are multifarious and comprehensive, but except in small matters relating to the maintenance of order he has no independence and no initiative, and he can take no action without the consent of the *jemâa*. He is chosen by the influential persons of the village (the choice being subject to ratification by the *jemâa*) and is always a member of one of the leading families, for although in principle any man may be Amin of his own village it is in fact necessary for him to be a wealthy man and one able to rely on the support of a powerful *sof* to uphold his authority. The Amin is aided by lieutenants whom he appoints to supervise the different quarters of the village and to keep him informed of all that passes.

The solidarity of its members is a marked feature in the life of the village; everyone is helped at need in his harvesting and field work by the members of his quarter or of the village in general, and a man wishing to build a house can claim the assistance of the village, contributed under an organized scheme. Provision for the needs of the poor is made from the public revenue. The unit is not the individual but the family, and so close is the tie that each member is liable for crimes committed by any one of them, while frequently the property of a family is left undivided and the revenue enjoyed by all its members in common.

The village—in other respects so isolated and self-centred—is brought into contact with its neighbours through an organization called the *sof*, a fraternity and mutual aid society. Each village is divided into two opposed *sof*, and as these are seldom equally matched numerically, it is common for them to ally themselves with similar fraternities in neighbouring villages, until the ramifications of the league may extend throughout entire districts. Within the village the claims of the *sof* rank above all personal interests, and even ties of kinship are violated if the honour of the fraternity is at stake. A man who is a member of a powerful *sof* can feel safe alike from the vengeance of individuals and from the justice of the law, and will be supported by his fellow-members with every resource from perjury to murder. But although loyal to his *sof* while a member of it, the devotion of the Kabyle is dictated entirely by self-interest, and he thinks little of transferring his allegiance from his own to another *sof* if he feels he is likely to gain thereby. Beyond the village the cohesion of the fraternity is somewhat weakened, and although in time of civil war members of a *sof* will freely supply money and provisions to fellow-members, and will extend unstinted hospitality to fugitives, they would expect to be paid at a suitable money rate for any armed contingent they might send. The leaders of the *sof* are generally members of wealthy and powerful families; to them is entrusted the administration of the funds (raised by member's subscription) from which they may disburse large sums on secret services without being called upon to render account of their stewardship.

Generally speaking the Berbers are good craftsmen, and their products are sufficiently well characterized to be distinctive. In architecture the use of straight lines, and in decorative enrichment the predominance of rectilinear geometrical designs, stand in evident opposition to the art commonly and conveniently, if rather inaccurately, described as 'Arab'. Thus the minarets of the Berber mosques are square, or sometimes hexagonal, contrasting profoundly with the circular form usual, e.g. in the Nile Valley, and this holds even for such world-famed structures as those of Marrakesh and Seville in Spain. Exceptions are to be found in the tomb shrines of holy men, for which the Arabic *qubba*, with its circular, sometimes octagonal, cupola has been adopted, and in the discreet use of the arc above entrances framed by straight lines. Berber pottery, as exemplified by the fabrics of Algeria, is perhaps more characteristic and has certainly been more closely studied than that of any other part of Africa. This is not to be attributed to any striking beauty of these wares but rather to the interest aroused by the suggestion that it is closely akin to that of the predynastic Egyptians. Without that discussion for which there is no space here, it is fair to say that Kabyle pottery shows sufficient resemblance to that of the proto-Egyptian as to go well with the survival of the proto-Egyptian physical type among the Berber peoples. Turning to the minor arts, the silver jewellery of Algeria, particularly of the Aures Mountains, is characteristic and distinctly beautiful, especially when enriched with coral or enamel. Embroidery and weaving have to a greater extent come under Arabic influence, but even here a number of different schools of Berber design still exist.

Although consideration of the doctrines of orthodox Muhammadanism falls outside the scope of the present work, there are two manifestations of Islam which have so greatly influenced the life of the peoples of North Africa that it would be improper to omit a short reference to each. The first of these, the doctrine of *baraka*, is common to Arabs and Berbers, and, indeed, exists wherever Islam is practised, but since it has developed to an overwhelming extent among the Berbers it will be considered in this chapter, while the other institution, namely the religious fraternities of North Africa, since its importance and development are greatest among the Arabs, will be dealt with in Chapter 10.

Literally the Arabic word *baraka* means 'blessing', but in North Africa it is used to denote a mysterious force, a blessed virtue, which is from God, and which is most nearly connoted by the English word 'holiness', so that the term as applied to persons possessing *baraka* in an exceptional degree may fairly be translated 'saint'. No man has ever possessed more *baraka* than the Prophet, and it is a portion of his *baraka* that is transmitted to the *shurifa* (sing. *sherif*), his descendants in the male line through his daughter Fatima. Apart from the *shurifa* the commonest possessors of *baraka* are the heroes who have fallen fighting for Islam, and local holy men owing their sanctity perhaps to their descent and partly to a reputation for miracles performed during their lifetime. A combination of the two forms of holiness exists in the *baraka* of the reigning Sultan of Morocco; he not only has the holiness that pertains to him as head of the family of 'shereefs' to which he belongs, but also that of the sultanship, i.e. of the 'Vicegerent of God on His earth', perpetually renewed to him by forty saints who every morning pass over his head. It is on the Sultan's *baraka* that the welfare of the country depends; when it is strong the crops are abundant, women give birth to healthy children, and the country prospers, and when in 1908 the sardine fishery was especially good this was attributed to the recent accession to the throne of a Sultan especially full of *baraka*. Others possessing much *baraka* who, though inferior to the *sherif*, form a kind of religious nobility, are the *marabtin* (*marabit* or *mrabit*), whence the origin of the French corruption '*marabout*', heard all over North Africa to signify any holy man. *Baraka* is essentially a transmissible virtue, one of the most effective methods being for the saint to spit into the mouth of anyone he wishes to benefit, while the same result may be brought about by the two eating food together before parting; in the latter case the holy man pronounces a traditional formula.

Of actual manifestations of *baraka* of social importance none is more striking than the sanctuary which is constituted by the shrines of saints. In one instance it is not only the area within the enclosing wall of the shrine, but the whole space lying between a series of cairns erected on spots from which the shrine becomes visible. Anyone who can see the tower of this saint's mosque is within his protection and so safe from every form of persecution. Such shrines often contain graves, and are then all the holier, the extraordinarily binding character of oaths sworn upon them being due to the *baraka* of their saint.

There is no limit to the miracles which take place at the shrines of saints, of whom many have the strongest objection to Christians and Jews. Thus Professor Westermarck—from whose work these remarks concerning *baraka* have been taken—was not allowed to approach one specially celebrated shrine, while, as is

well known, there is a little town on the Atlantic coast in Northern
Morocco which through its saints has long been kept free from
Christian residents, since all who attempted to live there became
ill and were obliged to leave. It cannot be over-emphasized that
baraka is extremely sensitive to external influences, by which it
may be polluted and lessened. It is confidently stated that one
reason why the Sultan Mulai 'Abdl'aziz lost his *baraka* was that
Christians frequented his court; so, too, the barbers of certain
out-of-the-way districts say that there is no *baraka* in the razors
of their colleagues in Tangier because they are sharpened by
Christians, and a prayer said in a Jewish or Christian house is of
no avail. Further, a Jew may not tread on a threshing-floor or
enter a granary, nor should he approach a beehive lest the bees
incontinently swarm.

The Tuareg (sing. Targui), also known as the Kel Tagulemust,
the People of the Veil, inhabit an extensive, unbroken territory
from Touat-Ghadames to northern Nigeria and from Fezzan to
Lac Faguibine west of Timbuktu. They consist of several groups
or confederations of clans. The main groups are: the Kel
Ahaggar (in the Ahaggar Mountains), the Kel Ajjer (on the
mountains of Tassili-n-Ajjer), the Kel Air (in the Air Mountains), the Kel Adrar (in the mountains of Adrar-n-Ilforas), the
Kel Geres (south of Air), the Iullemmeden (round Tahoua,
Menaka, and Gao), the Tenguereguif and the Kel Antassar
(round Timbuktu and Lac Faguibine). The first two groups are
known as the Northern Tuareg (8,000) and live in true desert
country breeding camels, goats, and sheep. The other groups,
known as the Southern Tuareg (235,000), live mainly in steppe
and savannah countries and also breed cows. Each group has a
supreme chief, the *amenokal*, elected by the leaders of the
composing clans, the *amenokal* of the People of Air being the
Sultan of Agades. The *amenokal* usually has little real authority
and his tenure of office is precarious; the succession, as that of the
chiefs of clans, though not strictly hereditary, normally passes to
the sister's son among the Northern Tuareg, while among some
southern groups (e.g. the Iullemmeden) succession to chieftainship is patrilineally determined.

The clans are divided into distinct classes, the most important of which are the 'nobles' (Imajeghen), and the 'servile' or 'vassal' class (Imghad). The chief of a noble clan is the leader in war and the dispenser of justice in peace, and in council with the heads of families he exercises authority over the Imghad clans associated with his people, through the chiefs of these servile groups. Some of the Imghad clans are rich and respected, and though they cannot change their allegiance and are bound to assist their overlords in time of war, they are in no sense considered as the property of the latter and are not expected to do menial work, all obligations being imposed collectively and not on any one Imghad. Both classes own slaves, most of whom live in their masters' camps to serve as herdsmen. Other black-skinned castes are found in Tuareg country. Among these are the blacksmiths (Enaden), who are much despised by the Tuareg, although they have a rather independent position. A man's status is governed by the class of his mother, so that should a man of the Imajeghen marry an Imghad woman the children will be servile. Among some Tuareg groups, however, children of such mixed marriages belong to a special class (Ereguenaten) which is considered neither noble nor servile. Though descent is matrilineal the government of each unit is patriarchal, and in the main similar to that of a nomad Arab tribe (see p. 153). Among most groups property is now inherited according to Islamic rules, and the patrilineal system of the Arabs tends to displace the old matrilineal Tuareg system also with regard to descent and succession.

The wearing of the veil (*tagulemust*) has assumed a ritual importance. In this veil the men live and sleep; they lift it up to eat, but when so doing hold their hand over the mouth. The veil consists of a long strip of cloth wound round the head so as to form a hood, and covering the mouth and nose, only a slit of about an inch wide being left in front of the eyes. The veil, which is the symbol of adult status, is adopted by young men when 15 to 20 years old. A similar piece of cotton (*alesjo*) used as a head-cloth is given to young women after the first occurrence of menstruation (in the north), or just before marriage (in the south). The women, however, never veil their faces like the men.

The Tuareg are a tall people. The noble class attains an average stature of 68½ inches, a figure definitely higher than that given for vassals or serfs. Small-boned, with no superficial muscular development, they have astonishing powers of physical endurance and bear themselves with great dignity and grace; their features are clear-cut, with a firm pointed chin, a broad, slightly retreating forehead, heavy brow-ridges, and prominent but not high cheek-bones, the whole profile somewhat accentuated. The skin is a reddish yellow, the eyes dark, the hair long, black, and wavy. As a group the 'noble' Tuareg are frankly dolichocephalic, with an index of just over 73, which is only slightly higher than that of a large 'mixed' group, and leptorrhine (N.I. 67-68). Moreover, though individuals with round or almost round heads exist, these are rare, and the Tuareg may be regarded as the most long-headed of the Northern Hamites.

Although the servile class shows no great difference in head shape or in stature, skin colour, hair, and the nasal indices do, however, indicate a considerably larger admixture of Negro blood, for though the averages do not greatly differ, there is a much greater straddle among the lower class; moreover, the skin is often darker and the hair may be spiralled, a character not noted among the nobles.

In character the Tuareg are independent, brave, impulsive, and mendacious, chivalrous to women and with a great love of poetry and music. They are a hardy and abstemious people, and before the coming of the French were notorious raiders—indeed raiding might be regarded as the national sport—pillaging outlying Arab settlements and raiding trade routes, only such caravans being safe as paid for passage and convoy. The characteristic weapons are sword, spear, and the arm-dagger, held on the arm by a ring. Tuareg craft, apart from mat-making and leather-working carried on by the women, is but little developed. Weaving is unknown, cooking-pots are acquired from settled agriculturists, and weapons and camel saddles are manufactured by the blacksmiths.

Monogamy is customary, and the position of the Tuareg women has no real parallel elsewhere among Muhammadans. They are held in great honour and allowed their entire liberty; it is the women who teach the children and are the repositories of learning and best versed in the traditions of the people. The liberty the Tuareg accorded to their women shocked that great traveller Ibn Batuta: commenting on the status of the Tuareg women, he describes how he visited one of his Tuareg friends and found him sitting on a carpet, while on a couch in the middle of the house was his wife, in conversation with a man seated at her side. 'I said to Abu Mohammed: "Who is this woman?" "It is my wife," he replied. "The individual with her, who is he?" "It is her friend." "And are you pleased at such a state of affairs, you who have lived in our countries and who know the precepts of Holy Writ?" "The relations of women with men in this country are good and are correct, they are right and honourable; they arouse no suspicion. Besides, our women are not like those of your country." ' Ibn Batuta adds: 'I was surprised at his stupidity. I left his house and never returned. . . .' A recent traveller sums up the position of women by quoting the Tuareg proverb: 'Men and women towards each other are for the eyes and for the heart, and not only for the bed.'

The frequent use of the cross in ornament may point to a survival of early Christian influence, but today the Tuareg are nominally Muslims, though lax in religious observance. As among most other Muslims, animism is part of everyday belief; it is commonly accepted that below the surface the desert is peopled by a class of supernatural beings who delight in playing mischievous pranks on the wayfarer, and all unexplained phenomena are referred to invisible agencies, while the mysterious droning or drumming heard on a still night in many parts of the desert is the voice of the jinn conversing among themselves.

The Tuareg alone among the people of North Africa possess an individual non-Arabic script, T'ifinagh. It is alphabetic, not syllabic, but owing to the abbreviations practised and to the absence of all vowels except 'a', it assumes a pseudo-syllabic quality and has come to resemble a sort of shorthand. The alphabet consists of from between twenty and thirty symbols, varying from place to place, in addition to about twelve ligatures of two or sometimes three letters. Among most tribes a knowledge of T'ifinagh is now confined to the older women and men, for although in olden days all the Tuareg knew how to write, and taught the children, the younger generation are largely illiterate. The holy men and scribes usually employ only Arabic. But although the script is often spoken of as Tuareg, and indeed is most highly devloped among them, this really signifies no more than that they alone use it at the present day; it is found far and wide in North Africa, where no Tuareg have ever been and where it must be regarded as Hamitic (or 'Libyan') in a wide sense; indeed inscriptions are particularly plentiful in the coastal region of eastern Algeria.

The Tibu, stated to be the direct descendants of the ancient Garamantes, inhabit the Tibesti massif from which they take their name, Ti-bu, 'Rock people'. Until ousted by the Senussi they also occupied the Oasis of Kufra. There are two sections, the northern Teda and the southern Daza, through whom the Tibu gradually merge in the Negroid population of the Central Sudan. This intermingling with the blacks dates from remote times, but the unmixed Tibu of the northern section are in the main Berbers, and although the type of the men is somewhat coarser than the Tuareg, that of the woman has been described as almost the finest in Africa. They were formerly a powerful people, and in the sixteenth century constituted a large proportion of the military force of the Kingdom of Kanem. They use the throwing knife, and until recently were at enmity with their neighbours the Tuareg. Although nominally converted to Islam in the eighteenth century many still practise heathen rites: thus, among the Baele during prayers addressed to Yido—the supreme being—a sacred stone is sprinkled with flour and with the blood of a sacrificed sheep.

The Fulbe, as they call themselves, are known by a number of terms (Peuls, Fula, Fellata, and Fulani). They are found throughout the Western and part of the Eastern Sudan, from Senegambia in the west to Chad in the east, and also in the highlands of the Cameroons. They may be nomadic pastoralists, semi-sedentary farmers and cattle owners, sedentary agriculturists, or, in some northern Nigerian Emirates, members of a ruling class.

The Fulani gradually spread their influence over the Western Sudan and Upper Senegal during the days of the Ghana Empire and had found their way into Hausaland by the end of the thirteenth century. Their conquest of that country dates from 1804, when reformist Muslims, led by a Fulani holy man, Usuman the son of Fodio, declared a Holy War against the overlords of the Hausa states whose adherence to Islamic belief and practice had lapsed. By 1810 Fulani domination was firmly established over the Hausa states, and Usuman was declared Commander of the Faithful, with his capital at Sokoto. By 1840, further Emirates were established, each under a Fulani governor owing ultimate allegiance to Usuman's successor. Until the establishment of British colonial rule, the Fulani Empire extended over what is now northern Nigeria, with the exception of Bornu and the more remote pagan areas.

As found today in West Africa, the mass of the Fulani population, numbering perhaps six millions, is disseminated among diverse Negro populations, but its main concentrations are found in Fouta Djalon in Guinea, Macina in Mali, and Adamawa in northern Nigeria. This population may be divided into three categories: the pastoral Fulani (often called Cattle Fulani or Bororo in the literature), the sedentary Fulani or Fulanin Gida, as they are called in Hausa, and the semi-sedentary Fulani.

The pastoral Fulani have a preponderance of non-negroid physical traits—straight hair, straight nose, thin lips, slight physique, and light reddish-brown skin colour; the women are distinguished by their beauty of countenance and graceful carriage. In character they are exceedingly reserved, distrustful, and shy, and noted for their dissimulation and finesse. The simple or compound family, which is the basic economic unit, depends for its livelihood on cattle. The basis of subsistence is milk, which is consumed in various forms or sold and exchanged in the markets for cereal foods. Milking and marketing are usually done by women and girls, herding and watering by men and boys. The animals are killed for meat on ceremonial occasions only. Pastoral Fulani also manage cattle owned by settled Fulani or wealthy Hausa, and have the benefit of the dairy produce together with a proportion of the progeny. Conversely, in some

areas pastoral Fulani employ herdsmen from the sedentary
Fulani or pagan communities. Their dwellings, which are allo-
cated to married women, are usually crude beehive huts, or
simple rectangular shelters, the main components of which may
be transported on pack animals when camp is shifted. Cattle are
corralled at night round a smudge fire near the shelters, sometimes picketed, with the calves tethered separately to a calf-rope.
Herds are trained to scatter into the bush at the herdsmen's
signal. The various myths of origin of cattle tell of a water-spirit
who brought cattle from a river to give to some Fulani who had
endured the rigours of the bush, on condition that whenever they
were corralled a smudge fire should be lit for them.

The intermediate category of semi-sedentary Fulani is made
up of pastoral Fulani who have recently or temporarily abandoned complete dependence upon cattle. It is not uncommon for
semi-sedentary Fulani to return to nomadic pastoralism when
their herds which have been depleted by disease increase
suitably, but more usually they become absorbed in the sedentary
population.

The sedentary Fulani are either communities of those who
have long ago abandoned pastoralism, or settlements of Negro
ex-slaves who speak the Fulani language and thus describe themselves as Fulani. In general the sedentary Fulani display more
Negroid physical features than do the pastoral or semi-sedentary
groups, owing either to their Negro origin or to long periods of
intermarriage and concubinage with their Negro neighbours.
Similarly, adherence to Islamic belief and ritual and conformity
with Islamic legal provisions are encouraged by the sedentary
life. Nevertheless Islam has affected pastoral Fulani too, particularly from the time of British colonial rule onwards, and today
it is likely that few of them could be described as pagan.

The Fulani speak a language (Fulfulde) which is important for
the understanding of many African language problems. Its classification has always been controversial. It was formerly classed
either as a Negro language (Delafosse) or as a primitive Hamitic
language (Meinhof); nowadays it is termed a West Atlantic language (Greenberg, Westermann, and Bryan, and others), its
greatest structural affinities being with Serer, Wolof, and

Biafada. Its most striking and anomalous structural feature links it with Bantu. This is a division of nouns into classes marked by suffixes with which pronouns have a recognized relationship. Twenty-eight such classes have been noted in the four or five main dialects of Fulfulde. Each class contains names of particular series of objects or categories though in a less heterogeneous way than in Bantu. Thus the suffix *am* is applied to liquids, e.g. *kosam* (milk), *ndiyam* (water); *o* or *jo* to humans, e.g. *ardo* (leader), *gaynaako* (herdsman); *el* to diminutives, e.g. *binngel* (child); etc. New vocabulary from African and non-African languages may be fitted into these classes, e.g. *Alhajjiijo*, cf. Arabic (a pilgrim to Mecca); *Ajjiaajo*, cf. Kanuri (a fief holder); *Diyojo*, cf. English (a District Officer); *motayel*, cf. English (a pick-up truck, lit. 'a small motor').

Giving due weight to classes such as these, and with reservations concerning the Bantu vocabulary, the view has been put forward that the origin of the Bantu languages is to be explained on the supposition that a language similar to Fulfulde was that of a dominant group in the midst of Sudanic-speaking peoples; and that the vocabulary of the latter being assimilated, traces of Fulfulde-like modes of thought and expression persisted in the new group of languages which we now speak of as Bantu.

7

Nilo-Hamites and Nilotes

As ALREADY STATED, the Hamites entered Africa—or, if the African hypothesis of their origin be maintained, entered Negroland—in a long succession of waves, of which the earliest may have been as far back as the end of the pluvial period. It is the purpose of this chapter to discuss some of the main results of the mixture of the Hamite with the Negro and to define some of the principal groups of mixed ancestry to which their invasions gave rise.

All these mixed populations are Negro-Hamitic, or hamiticized Negroes (though some of the members of the Bantu group carry but little Hamitic blood and show no great signs of Hamitic culture), with here and there no doubt some pygmy admixture. Until a better terminology is invented, based on more precise knowledge than is available at the present time, some such groupings as the following seems best; it must, however, be noted that the groups are defined by varying criteria, that owing to the lack of physical measurements language plays far too big a part, and that in this classification are included all the people commonly called Negroes, excepting only the true West African Negro and a few peoples provisionally excluded mainly because so little is known about them.

The mechanism of the origin of the Negro-Hamitic peoples will be understood when it is realized that the incoming Hamites were pastoral 'Europeans'—arriving wave after wave—better armed as well as quicker witted than the dark agricultural Negroes, for it must be remembered that there was no Bronze

Age in Africa, and we may believe that the Negro, who is now an excellent iron-worker, learnt this art from the Hamite. Diagrammatically the process may be described as follows. At first the Hamites, or at least their aristocracy, would endeavour to marry Hamitic women, but it cannot have been long before a series of peoples combining Negro and Hamitic blood arose; these, superior to the pure Negro, would be regarded with disdain by the next incoming wave of Hamites and be pushed farther inland to play the part of an incoming aristocracy *vis-à-vis* the Negroes on whom they impinged. And this process was repeated with minor modifications over a long period of time, the pastoralists always asserting their superiority over the agriculturists, who constantly tended to leave their own mode of life in favour of pastoralism or at least to combine it with the latter. The end result of one series of such combinations is to be seen in the Zulu, of another in the Ganda, while an even more striking result is offered by the symbiosis, to use a biological term, of the Huma of Ankole and the Iru. The Huma, a tall, cattle-owning aristocracy, with narrow noses and faces, so unlike the Negro (though they always have Negro hair) that Johnston when he first saw them thought they were Egyptian soldiers left behind by Emin Pasha, live in the country of the shorter, broader-faced Negro Iru; the latter normally provide them with grain, and no doubt in the past there has been intermarriage (witness the spiralled hair of even the Huma aristocracy), though at the present time each group is said to keep to itself.

These examples give a rough idea of the almost infinite variety within the great mass of hamiticized Negroes, so that it is not surprising that classification is difficult and its results often so doubtful that even main groups present an indistinct edge and the observer is compelled to fall back on the relatively easily determined facts of language. With this warning the following may be regarded as the primary divisions of the hamiticized Negro (Fig. 3, p. 103):

(1) The Nilo-Hamites.

(2) Nilotes, using the term in the rather narrow sense defined below (p. 111 f.).

(3) Bantu.

In this chapter we shall briefly describe Nilo-Hamites and Nilotes, leaving the great mass of Bantu Africa to Chapters 8 and 9.

The Nilo-Hamites are limited to East Africa and East Central Africa. They occupy much of Kenya, with that part of Uganda which runs northwards to the Sudan boundary, as well as some of the northern portion of Tanzania.

As already stated, they have arisen as the result of the mixture of Hamite with Negro, and as the name implies they have a considerable amount of Hamitic ancestry, i.e. definitely more than almost all the Bantu and Nilotes. This relative preponderance of the Hamitic side of their ancestry is reflected alike in speech, appearance, and culture. They all speak languages of Nilotic type, and although their skins are dark their faces are generally Negroid rather than Negro, the difference being especially obvious in the nose. Culturally they are predominantly pastoralists; indeed many of their tribes depend entirely on their herds, leading the semi-nomadic life that this entails. Apart from the criterion of language there are Bantu tribes that in one respect or another conform to the conditions just cited, e.g. many of the Bantu Kikuyu are no more pure Negroes than are the Nilo-Hamitic but sedentary Nandi, while the pastoralism of the Bantu-speaking Huma is at least comparable with that of the Nilo-Hamitic Masai. The Nilo-Hamites in fact speak Nilotic languages with Hamitic elements, and are predominantly pastoral Negroids; it may be added that their extreme range is from the neighbourhood of Lake Rudolph in Kenya in the north to 5° or 6° S. in Tanzania.

The chief tribes are the Masai, the Nandi group (comprising Nandi, Kipsigis or 'Lumbwa', Keyo or Elgeyo, Pokot—better known as Suk—Barabaig, and Dorobo), and the Teso group (Teso, Kuman, Karamojong, Turkana, and Toposa). All these tribes are moderately tall and slender, long-headed—though not so long-headed as the tall Negroids (Nilotes) of the Nile Valley, with whom affinities may be traced via the Lotuko and Bari—sometimes narrow-faced, and with noses (and indeed features generally) which are far removed from those of the true Negro.

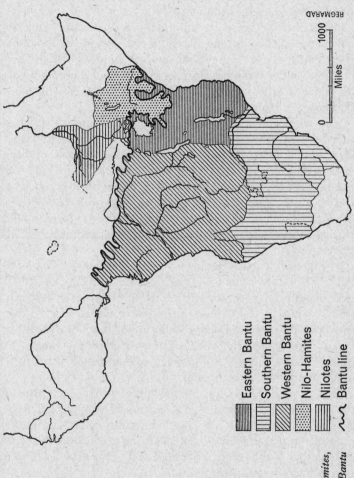

Fig. 3 *Nilo-Hamites, Nilotes, and Bantu*

Eastern Bantu
Southern Bantu
Western Bantu
Nilo-Hamites
Nilotes
Bantu line

The Masai, Nandi, Kipsigis, and Suk, perhaps because we know so little about the other Nilo-Hamitic tribes, are to be regarded as specially typical of the group.

Physically these tribes are tall, their average stature being 68 inches. Masai, Nandi, and Turkana give a cephalic index of 73–74, but the Suk are mesocephalic with an index of about 77. The noses of the Masai are narrower than those of the other tribes just cited, the Masai being mesorrhine, and the Nandi, Suk, and Turkana platyrrhine.

Ignoring for the purpose of description the changes that were forced on the tribes as the result of European colonization, the Masai and Turkana are nomadic herdsmen, as probably all their congeners once were, but at the present day the Kipsigis, hill Suk, and Teso are sedentary, leading an agricultural life in addition to owning cattle. The majority of the remaining tribes are best described as semi-nomadic and are doubtless on the way to becoming of fixed habitat, like the Nilotes, even if cattle remain their chief interest.

The men of the Nilo-Hamites for the most part wear very little clothing; girls and women wear well-dressed leather petticoats of some length, often edged with beads, and whenever they can afford it a great mass of brass wire in coils on the wrists and arms, and especially round the neck, coming low on the chest. The great majority, perhaps all these tribes, remove the lower incisors. The Masai and all the Nandi group practise clitoridectomy and, with minor exceptions, circumcision.

It is impossible to exaggerate the importance of their cattle to the Masai and kindred tribes; not only must their practical function be considered, but also their ceremonial value; indeed the prominence that grass has in ritual among these tribes is due to the fact that it is the food of their beloved animals. Hollis gives a translation of a Masai text:

As with people, each cow is known by name; there is a saying . . . one cow resembles a man's head . . . if a man has a cow which he looks after and it bears, it enables him to live, for he can marry and have children and thus become rich. . . . Whenever there is a drought the women fasten grass on their clothes and offer up prayers to God. . . . Whenever warriors return from a raid and it is desired to praise those who have killed some of the enemy, a girl takes a small gourd of milk and having covered it with green grass sprinkles it over them. . . . The Masai love grass very much, for they say, 'God gave us cattle and grass, we will not separate the things God has given us.'[1]

Among the Suk, and this may be true of the other tribes, cattle are so important that if an adjective stands by itself the noun it qualifies is always understood to be 'cow'. Again, in Suk even the skin of an ox has a different word from the skin of any other animal, and the verb 'to drink', if the fluid be milk, is different from the word meaning to drink any other liquid, while an ordinary gourd has a name different from that of one used to collect milk. Moreover, milk is so sacred among the Nandi, who it will be remembered are agriculturists as well as pastoralists, that special precautions are taken to prevent the mixing of milk and meat in the stomach; thus when meat has been eaten, no milk may be drunk for twelve hours, and then only after salt and water have been swallowed.

The Masai dwelling-hut, called *enk-aji*, is of a peculiar type, rather like a long, flat-roofed tunnel of brushwood and mud, divided into family compartments each with its own door; the whole is surrounded by a thorn fence, and the cattle herded within this at night. The Nandi and the agricultural Suk may be said to live in garden settlements, each man having his own homestead in or near his fields of grain. Near the huts are the granaries, and here and there the *sikiroinet*, the communal sleeping-places of the unmarried warriors. Here the unmarried girls visit the young men, staying with them for a few days at a time. No married women may sleep in these huts, which are looked after by the girls while their lovers are away at war or raiding. There is also an assembly, or club-house, frequented by the warriors and in which the old men drink beer. Youths and girls generally live in huts by themselves or with old women. A man will keep a few head of cattle near his house, but for most of the year the greater part of the cattle are herded on the grazing grounds, necessarily at some distance from the cultivation. Although the Nandi also were primarily herdsmen, with a mode of life resembling that of

[1] A. C. Hollis *The Masai* (1905).

the Masai, they are now capable agriculturists, though cattle-herding is still the chief occupation and interest of the men, and their attitude towards cattle is that of the Masai.

Among all these tribes, besides the ordinary functional divisions of boys, warriors, and elders, there is a well-developed system of age-sets. Among the Nandi all boys who are circumcised during a period of four years belong to a named age-set; within this those circumcised in one year form a division known as 'fire' from the fire in the hut where they were secluded during their initiation. There are seven set-names which recur in regular order. At the close of the four-year period initiates together enter the warrior grade and are expected to go out on cattle raids against the neighbouring tribes. Every fifteen years a great ceremony is held at which one warrior set formally hands over this responsibility to its successor. The date of this ceremony does not coincide with the completion of a new age-set, and in practice the new warriors begin their fighting life, and the older of their predecessors retire from active warriorhood, before it has been held. Thus there are periods during which members of two sets are in the warrior grade. The members of a single age-set often differ widely in biological age, since, though circumcision should ideally take place at puberty, each circumcision period is followed by an interval of ten or eleven years during which no initiations take place. All the adult bachelors, i.e. warriors, collect together, and the *orkoiyot*, chief 'medicine-man' (p. 107), strangles (some say slaughters) a white bullock; the meat is eaten by the men of the older age-set, each of the younger grade cutting a small ring from the hide and putting this on one of his fingers. The *orkoiyot* stands near a stool about which is heaped cow-dung studded with the fruit of a particular shrub. The members of the older age-set stand up, while the younger warriors, who are now receiving the control of the country, sit down. On a signal from the *orkoiyot* the outgoing age-set divest themselves of the warrior's skin and put on the fur garments of the elders. The new controllers of the country are then informed that the safety of the land and the welfare of the inhabitants are in their hands, and are solemnly warned to guard the land of their fathers.

Among the Masai the young warriors subsist entirely on milk, meat, and blood; they may not smoke, nor touch intoxicants. They live in their own villages with their mothers, some of their sisters, and immature unmarried girls who are their lovers. A man does not become an elder until he marries, which in old days might be postponed until he was over thirty.

There is no organization resembling age-sets among women, but the girls are instructed in their privileges and duties at the time that clitoridectomy is performed and during their period of seclusion.

In all these tribes the age-set must be looked upon not only as the organization by which the country is run, but also as the instrument of military operations, i.e. in the main, of raids, and it may be due to the respect which the Masai forays inspired that their customs appear to have been adopted to a considerable extent by such East African Bantu tribes as the Kamba, Taita, Kikuyu, and Chaga (p. 140).

Among the Nilo-Hamites the only office with potentially tribal association is that of the 'medicine man'. The Nandi *orkoiyot*, whose office and functions are similar to and derived from those of the Masai *olabaani*, is the principal medicine man and supreme chief of the race; he is a diviner and foretells the future, interprets dreams, and is skilled in the interpretation of omens and the averting of ill luck. The Nandi look to their *orkoiyot* for instruction when to plant their crops; he obtains rain for them; through him women and cattle are fruitful; and no war-party could expect to meet with success unless he approved of the expedition. It is obvious then that his powers and functions are much the same as those attributed by the Shilluk to their king (pp. 113–15); yet this parallel is not altogether true, for although the person of the *orkoiyot* is usually regarded as sacred, Kimnyole was clubbed to death by his own people in 1890 on account of the calamities— famine, sickness, and a raid in which 500 warriors perished—for which he was held responsible.

The Nilo-Hamites generally believe in a God associated with the firmament. By the Masai this being is known as Naiteru-Kop, the Beginner of Things, the Creator of the present order, though now, like so many African deities, he takes comparatively little interest in his world. In fact the word Eng-ai, a term used

E

indefinitely and impersonally but especially applied to the rain, the sky, and volcanoes, seems to be applied to the power to whom the Masai pray. We have rather more information concerning the Nandi: here the supreme deity is Asis, associated with the sun, who dwells in the sky, created man and beast, is acknowledged a benefactor, and to whom prayers are addressed. There are also gods associated with the thunder, who probably corresponds to Ilat—the rain—of the Suk. According to some accounts Ilat is himself the supreme God and Lord of life and death. But in fact the real force in Nandi religion is the ancestors, who are the mediators between man and Asis, and as such are the main-springs of the political structure as well. They are propitiated by offerings whenever necessary.

Of actual prayers we know little; perhaps the most precise information refers to the Nandi, among whom there is a definite attitude of prayer, the commonest petition running somewhat as follows:

'God, I beseech thee cover the children and the cattle; do I not approach thee morning and evening? ... Spirits of our ancestors, O guard us!'

And when the warriors are on a raid their mothers will spit towards the sun in the early morning, crying out, 'Asis, give us health!'

The Kipsigis, with the exception of some clans which expose the bodies to the hyenas, bury the dead of both sexes. Among both Kipsigis and Suk elderly males are buried in the cattle-pen. The Nandi bury all very old and very young dead. Otherwise the following is the normal Nandi practice. After death the body is carried at nightfall a few hundred yards to the north of the hut and placed on the ground, a man being laid on his right side, a woman on her left. When depositing the body the relatives cry: 'Hyenas, come and eat!' If on a visit on the fourth day after death the body has not been disturbed, a goat is killed and some of the meat placed on or near the corpse to attract the attention of the wild beasts, but should the latter still not come it is inferred that the deceased has been killed by witchcraft, and steps are taken to discover who is responsible. It is worthy of note that it is no part of the duties of the *orkoiyot* to determine who is guilty, and in this as in many other respects he differs notably from the 'witch-doctor' of the Bantu tribes of South Africa.

Although they are not true Nilo-Hamites it is convenient to give here (for the reasons set forth on p. 116), a short description of the Bari- and Lotuko-speaking tribes.

Physically the Bari are tall men with an average stature of 68 inches and a cephalic index of from 73 to 74, while the Bari-speaking tribes of the west bank are consistently shorter and rounder-headed, the height of Kakwa and Fajelu being about 66 inches with a cephalic index ranging round 76.

Of the social organization and beliefs of these west-bank Bari-speaking tribes we know little or nothing. Of the Bari of the eastern bank we can say that they are divided into a number of clans with patrilineal descent, some of these clans having such relationship to animals that it seems reasonable to suppose that they once had a totemic organization. Here again the rain-maker is the head of the tribe, though his position is very different from that of the divine king of the Nilotes, for when he failed to produce rain he was incontinently slain and a more satisfactory and competent ruler sought. Besides the rain-maker there are chiefs whose native name signifies 'father of the land' (pp. 36, 37), the term being applied to the man, or his descendants, who first cleared and planted a particular territory and who in virtue of this performs certain magical rites before sowing, during the growing of the crop, or before hunting. It is on account of their magical powers that these 'fathers' are of importance, since without them no success could be expected in hunting or garden-ing, and even fishing has its 'fathers'. The ceremonies to produce rain are rather elaborate, but the essential features seem to be the pouring of water and oil on to certain rain-stones—usually of quartz—and then the smearing of these with the contents of the stomach of a sacrificed goat. A summary account of the process ran as follows:

The rain-maker has certain green and white stones in a pot. He washes these in water and places them on a big stone [discovered later to be an old grindstone]. He smears the rain-stone with simsin oil and sacrifices a black goat near the stone. Then he, his assistants, and the old men eat of this and the rain comes.

It may be added that this ceremony would commonly take place
at the grave of a rain-making ancestor, or at a special shrine which
was probably associated with him.

The Lotuko-speaking tribes include the Lotuko and the
Lango. These tribes are dolichocephalic, with indices ranging
from 73 to something over 74, the Lotuko being tall, about 70
inches, while their congeners are some two inches shorter. They
are divided into totemic clans with patrilineal descent, the most
obvious feature of their totemism being the strongly held belief
that at death every individual becomes his clan animal. Almost
all that is known of these tribes applies especially to a particular
group of Lotuko, whose 'capital' is Tarangole. This community
has crocodile, monkey, elephant, white ant, and snake clans; of
these the crocodile is the most powerful, and to this clan its rain-
makers belong. Rain-making is an extremely complicated series
of ceremonies, and here again the chief part is played by rain-
stones, with certain sacred spears as subsidiaries, the water in
which these are laid being brought from a sacred pool where live
the crocodiles incarnating the rain-making ancestors.

The burial customs of this group are particularly interesting,
affording as they do an example of the rather widely spread belief
that the reproductive energy and prosperity of the people is in
some way associated with the digging-up of the bones of the dead,
which is done among the Lotuko from three to six months after
death. Another interesting feature is the very rapid burial
practised, followed by the construction of the *nametere*, an object
which can only be regarded as a very rough and degenerate
representation of the corpse, in connexion with which the first
mourning rites are held. It is difficult to resist the belief that the
nametere represents a last abortive attempt to preserve the corpse
for these ceremonies, in other words a once attempted but now
forgotten mummification.

The second great group of hamiticized Negroes are the Nilotes
(Fig. 3, p. 103), geographically limited to the Nile Valley or its
immediate neighbourhood, where they extend from some 200
miles south of Khartoum to Lake Kioga; one group, the Luo (or
ilotic-speaking Kavirondo, as opposed to the Bantu-speaking

Kavirondo), even reaching the north-east shores of Lake Victoria. Although they extend into Uganda, their centre is the Sudan, where they constitute by far the strongest of the racial units into which the blacks of the Nile Valley can be divided. But before describing the Nilotes it will be convenient to say something about the general racial problem presented by the Nile basin.

The Nilotes speak a Sudanic language, as do all the tribes of the Nile area; but within this great language family so many variations occur, even in the Nile Valley, that taking into consideration our relatively limited knowledge of physical characters, considerable interest attaches to Westermann's attempt to classify them on linguistic ground; it being understood that he uses the word 'Nilotic' to signify no more than 'appertaining to the Nile basin', while the anthropologist, as will shortly be clear, uses the term to signify a well-defined physical type associated with a particular culture. Westermann's classification is as follows:

1. The High Nilotic group, comprising Mittu, Madi, Abukaya, Abaka, Luba, Wira, Lendu, and Moru.

2. The Middle Nilotic group, comprising Shilluk, Anuak, Beir, Jur, Belanda, and many of the peoples of Eastern Uganda, Acholi, Lango, Aturu, and Jaluo.

3. The Low Nilotic group, comprising Dinka and Nuer.

It will be noted that this classification, though of wider geographical scope, yet embraces the whole area of the Sudan, although the Bari, with their numerous 'sub-tribes', and the Lotuko-speaking tribes are not mentioned. Westermann classifies the former with the tribes called Nilo-Hamites in this volume, i.e. with the Masai, Turkana, etc., to which he would also assign the Lotuko-speaking tribes. With this grouping before us we can delimit the Nilotes in the racial sense as comprising, among other peoples, the Shilluk, Anuak, Lango, Luo of the Bahr-al-Ghazal and of Kenya, the Dinka, and the Nuer. The Acholi and Belanda no doubt are of Nilotic origin, but in the former certainly and perhaps in the latter the physical characters have been modified by mixture with a foreign stock or stocks, and this may be true of the Lango. In the High Nilotic linguistic group the majority of Westermann's constituents, with the possible exception of the Madi, constitute a little-known group of inter-Congo-Nile tribes which have yet to be investigated.

Physically the Nilotes—whose most typical representatives are the Shilluk and Dinka—are tall, 'black' dolichocephals, with an average stature of 70 inches or perhaps a little over, and very long heads with a cephalic index of about 72. The Hamitic element may be strongest in the Shilluk, among whom it is not uncommon to meet men with clear-cut features, including prominent foreheads, thin lips, noses with high bridges, and nostrils that are by no means flaring. Indeed the majority of Shilluk are very obviously Negroid rather than Negro, while in spite of their dark skin and their no doubt preponderant Negro blood the Nilotes are culturally far more Hamitic than Negro, being so essentially pastoral that it is a commonplace that the Dinka generally fail to grow even enough grain to keep themselves comfortably in meal and beer from one harvest to another.

The men for the most part go naked, and even where this is not the case the genitals are left uncovered; the women wear leather aprons in front and behind. The lower incisors are generally removed, and cicatrices on the forehead are the rule; these probably are, or at one time were, tribal marks. In contradistinction to their neighbours on the Congo side of the Nile-Congo divide (p. 56) human sacrifice is very rare and cannibalism is unknown. Psychically the Nilotes show an aloofness and pride of race, with a lack of desire for European clothes or trade objects which is probably unparalleled elsewhere in Africa. Their predominant pastoralism is reflected in the almost religious esteem in which they hold their cattle. Among the Dinka there is a well-defined initiation ceremony at which the father of the young man presents his son with a bull, and it is no exaggeration to say that the youth attaches himself so strongly to this animal that the process called by psychologists 'identification' takes place; he will pass hours singing to and playing with his bull, he will be known to his associates by the name of his bull, and the death of the latter is a true bereavement. It is not then surprising that cattle are not killed for meat except on ceremonial occasions, the diet of the Nilotes being mainly milk and grain. As among the pastoral tribes of South Africa, women, except among the Dinka and Nuer, have practically no dealings with the cattle during the period of their sexual life, the care of the animals being entrusted entirely to the men and boys.

The broad spear is the typical weapon of the Nilotes, though some Dinka in the west of the Bahr-el-Ghazal have bows and arrows, presumably borrowed from their non-Nilotic neighbours. The Dinka of the Sudd and some of the Nuer are great hunters of the hippopotamus, its flesh forming a considerable part of their diet.

The social organization of the Nilotes varies from tribe to tribe. The Dinka present a congeries of tribes, not only occupying the banks of the Nile but extending far into the basin of the Bahr-el-Ghazal, all independent and with no evidence of ever having come under one leader. They have a clan organization with patrilineal totems. The less numerous Shilluk (though they number some 100,000) are united into a strong nation with a king who is supreme spiritual and temporal head, and if they ever were totemistic in the typical sense in which the Dinka are, this is not so at the present day. One of the functions of the Shilluk king and of the Dinka tribal headman is to make rain, so that they belong to that class to which Sir James Frazer applied the term of 'Divine King'. It is on account of the typical character of the divine kingship among these tribes, and the part which its existence among them has played in our knowledge of this institution, that somewhat undue space must be allotted to the subject.

Our knowledge is most complete with regard to the Shilluk king. Formerly he was not allowed to go into battle, and even now he keeps up considerable state and retains much of his old authority, while he is officially allowed an armed bodyguard. He rules his people from Fashoda (about eight miles from the Fashoda of history, of which the true name is Kodok), and no more eloquent evidence of his power can be offered than the imposing artificial mound upon which stands his homestead. To understand the divine nature of the king it is necessary to digress to the beginnings of the Shilluk nation. This traces its origin to one Nyakang, who, with his followers, split from the parent stock, then inhabiting part of the eastern Bahr-el-Ghazal, and, wandering forth and conquering as he went, was strong enough to found a dynasty and nation. Nyakang is the true culture hero of the Shilluk, and like so many great men (for he must be regarded as historical, and probably lived in the early seventeenth century) he did not die but vanished in a great wind. Semi-divine or divine honours have been paid to him since his disappearance, and in each king his spirit is supposed to be immanent, this immanence being at once the origin of and the reason for the kingly prerogative. As incarnating the spirit of Nyakang it is the king who is considered to be ultimately responsible for the well-being of his country and his people, and it was in order that the spirit might be housed in a thoroughly healthy body that the habitual practice of the Shilluk was to slay their king directly he showed signs of ill-health, or even of such gradual senescence as was evidenced by inability to satisfy his large number of wives. For it was felt that if the divine spirit were to inhabit a body that was not fully vigorous this lack of vigour might be communicated to the immanent spirit itself, and that, with the diminishing vitality of the king, the cattle would sicken and fail to bear their increase, the crops would rot in the fields, and men, stricken with disease, would die in ever-increasing numbers. Before discussing the death of the king and the installation of the new ruler it is necessary to point out that the spirit of Nyakang enters the king at his installation; there is no question of the congenital presence of the divine spirit, nor is the immanence of Nyakang in any strict sense comparable to the *baraka* of the holy men of Islam described in Chapter 6.

According to Shilluk folk-lore there was once a period when any man of the royal family who could slay the king might reign in his stead, and this is given as the origin of the practice that the king sleeps by day and is awake at night, for it was only at night, when alone or with his women, that his life might have been attempted with hope of success. The Shilluk tell of grim fights around the huts of the royal wives, neither the king nor his assailant calling for assistance, for it was said to be a point of honour for the matter to be settled in single combat. Many Shilluk give some such account, but it is certain that this was not the practice in recent times, when the leading part in killing the king was taken by members of certain families, called *ororo*, said to be descendants of the third Shilluk king. Perhaps in quite recent times the king was strangled, certainly a few generations ago he was walled up in a hut and allowed to perish. Whichever process was adopted there was an interregnum of some months after his death. An effigy of Nyakang was then brought to Fashoda from a shrine at Akurwa near the northern limit of the Shilluk country. The messengers also brought with them a four-legged stool, said to have belonged to Nyakang, and the central act of the installation of the new king was the placing of the effigy of Nyakang upon the stool for a short time, the king seating himself in its place immediately the effigy was withdrawn. It would seem that this part of the ceremony can have no other purpose than the transmission of the spirit of Nyakang to the new king, and this, the only example known in which there is direct evidence of the transmission of the spirit, affords the most interesting testimony to the perspicacity of Frazer, who in the first edition of *The Golden Bough* (published in 1890) pointed out that the ceremony at Nemi, upon which he based his conception of Divine Kings, implied the passage of something which might well be regarded as a divine or semi-divine spirit.

As might be expected, the Shilluk king is responsible for the great rain ceremony at Fashoda, when, through Nyakang, the God in the Firmament is adjured to send rain, and the king's representatives perform this and other important ceremonies in his provincial areas.

The rain-makers of the Dinka—equally divine kings—were not killed until so old that they themselves suggested this course, believing that they were no longer fit to advise or lead their people. The rain-maker would then lie on a stretcher and allow himself to be placed in the grave which had already been prepared for him; there he would remain for perhaps twenty-four hours, from time to time reciting accounts of his deeds and giving advice to the tribesmen who crowded around. Then, when his strength was failing him and he felt that he had no more to say, he would tell his people to cover him, and he would soon suffocate. It was considered absolutely necessary that this course should be taken: a Dinka rain-maker when asked whether he would not prefer to die a natural death indignantly repudiated the idea, pointing out that if he were not killed ceremonially his son could not succeed him and the tribe would lack a rain-maker.

South of the Dinka both banks of the Nile are occupied by a number of tribes speaking dialects of the Bari language. The true Bari have commonly been classed as Nilotes, and they do in some respects resemble the Dinka, with whom no doubt their northern sub-tribes, especially the Shir, have mixed to a certain extent. Yet on the whole their kinship is rather with the Nilo-Hamitic tribes of East Africa, and like these they speak a Hamitic language, though they cannot themselves be described as Nilo-Hamites. This is equally true of a group of tribes lying eastwards of the Bari, all speaking dialects of a common language and who from the name of their best known tribe may be called the Lotuko-speaking peoples. Short accounts of both Bari and Lotuko have been given on pp. 109–10.

8
Bantu

THE BANTU are a congeries of peoples, belonging predominantly to Central and Southern Africa, named from and defined by the peculiar type of language that they speak, which is generally considered to have originated in the neighbourhood of the Great Lakes. Apart from the interlacustrine Bantu (p. 137) the infusion of Hamitic blood which differentiates them from the true Negro is strongest in the east and south, weakest in the west and north. Thanks to the amount of study that has been given to the Bantu languages it is possible to draw a line representing the Bantu boundary with tolerable accuracy (Fig. 2, p. 9). Though it is less easy to define it in words, an attempt leads to some such result as the following.

Starting in the west from the sea coast at the mouth of the Rio del Rey (separating southern Nigeria from the Cameroons) the line runs north-east along the frontier, thence south and east with many irregularities to the south-east corner of the Cameroons. From here it passes eastwards across the two Congos, south of the River Uele to the head of Lake Albert. It crosses Lake Kioga, passing south of the peak of the Elgon to follow the eastern hinterland of Lake Victoria to its south-eastern corner. Thence it passes irregularly across Tanzania, northwards to the hinterland of Mombasa, whence a long narrow enclave runs north-west to Mt. Kenya, crosses the River Tana and runs northwards to the mouth of the Juba River, including between these two rivers only a narrow coastal zone.

The Bantu, who are defined on purely linguistic criteria, thus occupy the southern two-thirds of black Africa, and the term primarily implies no more than that the tribes included speak languages characterized by a division of nouns into classes distinguished by their prefixes (usually 12–15), absence of grammatical sex-gender, and the existence of alliterative concord, the prefix of each class (noun-class) being repeated in some form or another in all words agreeing with any noun of that class in the sentence. It is the reappearance of the prefix in every word in agreement with the noun that gives the alliterative effect known by this term. Hence the prefixes of any given class or 'principiation' of nouns will reappear with every adjective, verb, or pronoun agreeing with the noun, as may be illustrated by the Zulu sentence:

Umu-ntu w-etu omu-hle u-ya-bonakala si-m-tanda
  Man   our handsome he appears we him love.

Umu is the singular prefix of the class to which the word *ntu*, man, belongs, the plural prefix being *ba* (the initial vowel according to Meinhof is a later addition), so that in the plural the sentence just given will run:

Aba-ntu b-etu aba-hle ba-ya-bonakala si-ba-tanda
 People our handsome they appear we them love.

For other details concerning the Bantu languages the reader is referred to Professor Werner's book, mentioned in the bibliography, from which the example quoted is taken.

Even more simply the Bantu might be defined as all those Africans who use some form of the root *ntu* for human being; with the plural prefix this becomes *ba-ntu* (Bantu), i.e. 'the men [of the tribe]', whence the term under which the whole great group has passed into anthropological literature.

Although the Bantu are delimited on linguistic criteria, yet where Bantu and non-Bantu tribes are neighbours it may be found that certain physical qualities are to such a degree characteristic of each linguistic group that within particular areas a terminology based on language also serves to differentiate physical groups. The Cameroons (p. 130) offer an example. Apart, therefore, from its linguistic value the term Bantu when locally applied may come to have a fairly precise physical significance (and this argument applies to a greater or lesser extent to most of the other great families of Africa with a linguistic terminology).

On a basis primarily of geographical distribution, but taking into account cultural and, to a lesser extent, historical factors, the Bantu may be grouped as follows:

(I) Eastern Bantu, stretching from Uganda in the north, through Kenya, Tanzania, Zambia, Malawi, and Mozambique north of the Zambezi.

(II) Southern Bantu, south of the Zambezi and Kunene Rivers; a vast region including Rhodesia, the southern half of Mozambique, east and central parts of the Republic of South Africa, Swaziland, Botswana, Basutoland, and South-West Africa.

(III) Western Bantu, from the Atlantic north of the Kunene River to north-west Zambia and the Rift Valley (the line of the Great Lakes), and extending in the north-west to Gabon and the southern Cameroons.

It must, however, be realized that this classification, though useful, is so rough as to suffer from oversimplification. The Eastern Bantu fall naturally into three divisions: (a) Northern or interlacustrine, in Uganda and north-west Tanzania, grouped round Lake Victoria; (b) North-Eastern, mainly limited to Kenya; and (c) Eastern, occupying the remainder of the area (I) cited above. The Southern Bantu are composed of four divisions, delimited on pp. 120-1, while the Western Bantu should be regarded as composed of Central and Western divisions.

Of the three main groups of Bantu, the Southern and Western are spread over the largest areas and numerically are by far the most important. Yet of the latter we know comparatively little, indeed it is of the Southern and interlacustrine Bantu only that we can be said to have any considerable organized knowledge, and even here this applies only on the sociological side, since once more it must be emphasized that published physical measurements are almost entirely lacking. Somewhat illogically then we shall begin our account of the Bantu by considering the Southern group; only after this shall we briefly describe some of the best known tribes of the other groups and allude to such of their cultural features as are particularly interesting.

The Southern Bantu easily outnumber all other groups of the native inhabitants of South Africa and are about four times as numerous as the European population of the country. In the Republic of South Africa itself they number over ten million (1960), reaching a total of over fourteen million if the population of Basutoland, Swaziland, Rhodesia, Botswana, and South-West Africa be included, with roughly another million in Mozambique south of the Zambezi River. These Southern Bantu are divided politically into a very large number of tribal units, each with its own distinctive name but without any general or collective names of their own embracing closely allied peoples. In mode of life, social organization, and religious system all the Southern Bantu show certain broad resemblances, but in details of history, language, and various aspects of culture there are a number of important differences, which permit of their being classified into four main groups:

(IIa) Northern. The Shona peoples of Rhodesia and of Mozambique immediately south of the Zambezi as far as the Sabi River; their main linguistic subdivisions are the Zezuru, Manyika, Karanga, Kalanga, Korekore, and Ndau.

(IIb) Eastern. Chiefly in the coastal region south and east of the Drakensberg Mountains, extending from about the Sabi River on the north into the Cape Province in the south. This group consists of two main subdivisions, Nguni and Tsonga. The former include the Cape Nguni of the Ciskei and Transkei (Xhosa, Thembu, Mpondo, etc.), together with the 'Fingo', fugitive remnants of tribes broken up in Natal during the great inter-tribal wars at the beginning of the nineteenth century; the Natal Nguni, or 'Zulu' of Natal and Zululand, with their off-shoot the Ndebele (Tebele) of Rhodesia; the Swazi of Swaziland and the eastern Transvaal; and the 'Transvaal Ndebele' of central and northern Transvaal. The Tsonga, sub-divided into Tsonga, Ronga, and Tswa, are found chiefly in Mozambique, with offshoots in eastern and northern Transvaal.

(IIc) Central. Occupying the greater portion of the high plateau north of the Orange River and to the west and north of the Drakensberg Mountains. This group also consists of two main divisions, Sotho and Venda. The former includes the Southern

Sotho of Basutoland and adjoining districts, the Tswana
(Tlhaping, Rolong, Hurutshe, Kwena, Ngwaketse, Ngwato,
Tawana, Kgatla, etc.) of Botswana and western Transvaal, and
the Northern Sotho (Pedi and many others) of central and
northern Transvaal. The Venda are a very homogeneous group
occupying the Soutpansberg district of north-eastern Transvaal.

(IId) Western. Comprising the Herero and Ambo in the central
and nothern districts of South-West Africa. Both peoples are
divided politically into several distinct tribes, though under
German rule the Herero were united under one paramount chief.

As already stated, the classification given above is based
primarily upon considerations of language and culture, both
exhibiting appreciable differences as between the groups.
Physically, the Southern Bantu also present a great variety of
types: all are essentially Negroes, but since they have a varying
amount of Hamitic blood and have further mixed to a varying
extent with Bushmen and other peoples they naturally show a
diversity in their physical characters. Yet certain Negro characteristics predominate, especially the character of the hair. They
are, as a rule, well built, with strong muscular figures, and
graceful bearing and gait, especially noticeable in the women,
who are accustomed to carry loads on their heads. Tall individuals
are often seen, especially among the eastern tribes, but it appears
from a series of measurements taken of mine-labourers in
Johannesburg that on the average the Bantu of South Africa are
of medium height, nor does there seem to be any noticeable
difference in stature between the various tribal groups, as the
following figures demonstrate:

	ft.	in.
East Coast Natives (Tsonga, Chopi, Shangana) (1337)	5	6½
'Kaffirs' of Cape Province (630)	5	6¼
Natives of Rhodesia, mostly Shona (199)	5	5½
Sotho of Transvaal (521).	5	6
Sotho of Basutoland (79).	5	6½
Tswana (66)	5	5½
Herero (41)	5	6½

The complete measurements (given in a MS. by Turner,
deposited at the Royal Anthropological Institute) show that

4,098 South African Bantu of all groups and above the age of 21 years had an average height of about 5 feet 5¾ inches.

In skin colour the range is from the black of the Swazi to the yellowish-brown of some of the Tswana, the latter pointing to a by no means negligible amount of intermixture with Bushmen and Hottentots. The prevalent colour, however, is a dark choco-late, with a reddish ground tint. The hair is uniformly of the ordinary Negro type, short and typically characterized by numerous, often interlocking spirals. The head is generally dolichocephalic; the eyes usually big, black, and prominent; the nose varies—generally low and broad, it sometimes has a well-formed bridge and relatively narrow nostrils. The face is moder-ately prognathous, the forehead prominent, cheekbones high, lips thick and fleshy. There is, as a rule, little hair on the face, and the beard does not come until the middle twenties. Baldness is rare, but some tribes shave the head periodically.

The Negro facial type predominates in all groups, but side by side with it less characteristic features are sometimes seen, especially in the eastern group (*supra*, group II*b*), chiefly in the Zulu and the Tsonga sections, where narrow faces, thin lips, and prominent noses, strongly reminiscent of the Hamitic facial type, occur, and it is said that it is usually these natives who are of more than average height. Among the Zulu this type is said to con-stitute about 5 per cent. of the population. Among the Herero (*supra*, group II*d*)—not the Ambo—the Hamitic strain may be seen in the long face, long, narrow, straight nose, and relatively thin lips found in many individuals with long and lanky build and angular shoulders. Again, in the lighter-coloured groups of Tswana the short angular faces of the Bushmen are often met with, usually in individuals of lankier and weaker bodily build. Such divergent characters illustrate to some extent the nature of the physical strains which have modified the original Negro blood of the Bantu peoples.

Various forms of bodily mutilation are practised. Circum-cision, as part of puberty ceremonies, occurs in all the Central tribes, in the Xhosa section of the Eastern group, and in the Western tribes. It formerly existed among the other sections of the Eastern group (Zulu, Tsonga, and Fingo) as well, but seems to have been given up about a century ago, and none of these tribes now practises it, nor is it known to have ever occurred in the Shona tribes. An equivalent operation on girls, the exact details of which are hard to determine, exists apparently only in the Central tribes. Mutilations of the teeth, either filing to a point or extraction, are found in the Western tribes, in the Tsonga section of the Eastern group, and in a few of the more northerly and easterly Shona tribes (group IIa). Cicatrization is wide-spread, especially in the Eastern and Northern tribes; how far it exists as a common practice in the other groups is difficult to determine. Finally may be mentioned the practice of amputating part of one of the fingers, as a rule a terminal joint only. This practice occurs only in the Zulu and Xhosa tribes, although it is also found outside the Bantu, among the Bushmen and Hottentots, from whom it has probably been borrowed. Some of these forms of mutilation, especially circumcision and the extraction or filing of the teeth, are connected with puberty ceremonies; others seem to be merely ornamental.

Politically the Southern Bantu are grouped into a very large number of tribes, a tribe being defined for this group as a community, the members of which form a social and political organization under the government, control, and leadership of a chief, who is the centre of tribal life. Each tribe has its own name, and, as long as it is independent, its own territory.

The Southern Sotho (group IIc), mainly in Basutoland but overlapping into the neighbouring regions, are made up of fractions and remnants of a large number of tribes, mostly off-shoots of the Kwena, and are thus actually of Tswana stock. It is little more than a hundred years since these tribes were welded together by the great chief Moshesh to form the 'Basuto nation', so important a political unit that it is customary to regard it as a distinct section. The Pedi (an offshoot of the Kgatla) also attained political importance under their chiefs, Sekwati and Sekukuni, in the middle years of last century, and together with several smaller tribes which they dominated must now be regarded as a distinct section of the Sotho division.

The inhabitants of Natal and Zululand (group IIb), divided originally into more than a hundred small separate tribes, each with its own name, are all now collectively known as 'Zulus', a name derived from one of the tribes which, under the domination of Shaka, i.e. in the early years of the nineteenth century, absorbed and conquered most of the others and so formed the Zulu nation which played so important a part in the political history of South Africa in later years. Other tribes in this section of historical prominence and importance, still represented in Natal and Zululand, are the Tetwa, Ngwane, Baca, and Bomvu.

Bearing in mind the history of Shaka and his Zulu it is easy to see that the history of south-eastern Africa is a tangled skein of secessions, wars, migrations, and exterminations, giving rise to new tribal units, such as the Kololo (p. 148). Two more important instances are offered by the Ndebele and Ngoni (IIb). In 1819 Shaka defeated Zwide, chief of the Ndwandwe. Some segments of the Ndwandwe became part of the expanding Zulu state, others moved off to the north.

About 1821 Zwangendaba, who had been for a time a sub-chief of Zwide, led a party of refugees north-eastwards into the region of Delagoa Bay.... [There he] found Soshangane, a classificatory brother of Zwide, fighting with Nxaba, another minor chief, both of them [also] refugees from the rising power of Shaka. All three parties raided the indigenous Tsonga peoples and made captives fight alongside their new masters. Zwangendaba ... moved on farther north [and] in 1835 ... crossed over to the north side of the River Zambesi....

A few years after Zwangendaba left Natal, he was followed by Mzilikazi, a chief who for a while fought under Shaka and then fled from him with his followers. They became known as the Rhodesian Ndebele or Matabele.... The Maseko Ngoni [afterwards] broke away from Mzilikazi....

In about 1845 Zwangendaba died. ... Ntabeni, the regent, died shortly afterwards and his segment ... broke off from the rest of the group.... [They] went north on the east side of Lake Tanganyika and eventually settled in Kahama District.... A follower of Zwangendaba called Zulu Gama ... led his segment off to the east, where in the vicinity of Songea he met [the] Maseko Ngoni. ... Soon they split apart. Some people stayed on in Songea District, others went south and eventually rounded the southern end of Lake Nyasa to arrive in the Dedza District of southern Nyasaland, where they remain today. ... Mpezeni, with [his] segments, went south and eventually arrived

in Fort Jameson District. . . . The remainder moved off to the south-
east [into northern Malawi].[1]

Tribes vary enormously in size, some having from a few hundred
to at the most a couple of thousand members, as in the case of
most of the Tsonga, Shona, and Transvaal Tswana tribes, while
others are much larger: e.g. in the Tswana section (II*c*) the
Kwena of the Bakwena Reserve number about 40,000, the
Tawana 39,000 ,and the Ngwato 100,000; of the Ambo tribes
(II*d*) the Ndonga have 65,000 and the Kwanyama 55,000 members; the Swazi, again, number 180,000, and the 'Basuto' of
Basutoland (II*c*), who are by far the largest of all and might more
fairly be called a nation, number well over half a million.

The members of the Eastern, Northern, and Western groups
usually live in small settlements, which are scattered irregularly
over the country at some little distance apart. Each of these
settlements, or kraals, as they are commonly called in South
Africa, is inhabited by the members of a single domestic or household group, so that in these tribes the household group is also the
local group. In the Central tribes, on the other hand, the people
tend to collect together in villages or towns embracing a number
of different household groups. In Basutoland these villages are
numerous and generally fairly small, containing from five to fifty
households. In Botswana the people of each tribe live in an
irregular aggregation of numerous household groups, clustering
closely together and constituting a large town often of considerable size. Thus Kanye, the chief town of the Ngwaketse, has a
population of 23,000, and Serowe (Ngwato) 16,000.

But every household, whether it be a distinct local unit or
merely part of a larger village or town, is clearly marked off from
the rest, and in most tribes the household groups are all arranged
on the same definite plan. The central feature is the cattle-fold, a
circular enclosure which is fenced in strongly and in which the
cattle, sheep, and goats are kept at night. Around this at a regular
interval apart are ranged the huts of the various members of the
household. Among the Herero and all the Eastern tribes, with the
exception of the Tsonga section, these huts are of beehive shape;

[1] J. A. Barnes, *Politics in a Changing Society*, pp. 7, 16f., 21ff.

in all the other tribes (Ambo, Central group, Northern group, and Tsonga) they are round, with conical roofs. Each hut generally has its own small private yard where the cooking is done; there is also either a tree, a forked stick, some stones, or some other special spot which serves as an ancestral altar. The forked stick may be in a hut, at the entrance of the chief hut, or at the main gateway of the kraal itself. There is generally a common open space, and usually an enclosure reserved for the men, while the whole kraal may be surrounded by a circular, oval, or horse-shoe shaped enclosure or fence, made in a variety of ways.

Among the Eastern, Northern, and Central groups of the Southern Bantu the clans are organized on a patrilineal basis; in the Western tribes, on the other hand, the Ambo clans are matrilineal, while the Herero have a double system of organization by which everyone belongs to two units, one with patrilineal, the other with matrilineal descent.

In all the Eastern tribes the persons belonging to a clan bear a common *isibongo*, a word which may be translated 'praise name' or 'ancestral name' and is used for the name of the group. All members of an *isibongo* claim descent from a common ancestor in the male line, and the *isibongo* is usually the name of this ancestor. Thus a group whose *isibongo* is Tshezi all claim to be direct descendants in the male line from Tshezi, and are collectively known as amaTshezi; and a member of this group will often be addressed as 'Tshezi'. The *isibongo* of such a group is used as an honorific to or of the members of the group; it is a compliment or form of politeness to address a man not by his personal name but by his *isibongo* name, and under certain circumstances no other form of address is permissible.

A common *isibongo* imposes various obligations and rights upon the persons thus connected; in the first place, people with the same *isibongo* may not intermarry, i.e. marriage is permitted only between persons with different *isibongo*. Again, people may drink milk only with people bearing the same *isibongo* as themselves. Among the Zulu and Mpondo, to drink milk with a member of another clan is tantamount to pledging blood-brotherhood with that clan, and would prevent a man from marrying any of its women. There are further special taboos in some of the sections of this group, especially the Zulu, pertaining to each *isibongo*. Our knowledge of these taboos is somewhat inadequate. Although no marriage is possible between members of the same clan, a clan will often break up, a younger branch becoming a new clan and taking some more immediate ancestor as its *isibongo*, when intermarriage between the two groups can take place.

The Central tribes are also divided into groups, the members of which have a common name, the *seboko*, serving as cognomen and as a ceremonial and laudatory form of address. The *seboko* is not the name of a common ancestor but—and this holds also for the Northern tribes—is that of an animal or some mineral, such as iron, or some natural phenomenon, such as rain. It appears also that there were formerly various taboos and observances, ritual songs and dances, in connexion with the species of animal or object whose name is the *seboko* of a group.

For their subsistence the Southern Bantu depend principally upon pastoralism and hoe-culture. They keep cattle, sheep, and goats, which supply them with much of their food, in the form of milk, which is drunk sour, and with the raw material, in the form of skins, for some of their industries. The cattle are rarely killed for food save upon ceremonial occasions, meat being obtained chiefly by hunting. In addition crops are cultivated by all the tribes with the exception of the Herero. The crops raised are chiefly millet and maize, supplemented by vegetables such as pumpkins, peas, and beans. The cattle are herded and milked by the men, while the care of the fields is in the hands of the women, who are prohibited by religious sanction from having anything to do with the cattle. Only among the Herero do we find that the women do the milking, and in this they are exceptional not only among the Bantu tribes but among Negro-Hamitic peoples generally.

Ancestor worship forms the basis of the religious life of the Bantu. It is primarily a family cult, and is everywhere patrilineal —a man worships his own ancestors in the male line, and these are the only relatives whom he can ever approach. The head of the family conducts the worship, and, whatever its origin, the most obvious function of ancestor worship is to maintain the social

bond of the family and to keep the other members of the family
subordinate to the head, who alone has the power to intercede
with the dead; thus, among the Tsonga, when two brothers have
quarrelled the younger will perform a special sacrifice of recon-
ciliation with the elder in order that the latter may once more
intercede on his behalf with the ancestral spirits. The only
exception to the domestic nature of the cult is that the ancestors
of the chief are the source of strength for the whole tribe, for just
as the chief and his family guide the fortunes of the living, so his
ancestors care for the whole people of their ruling descendant.
Only members of the chief's family, however, can approach them
on behalf of the tribe as a whole, and thus it is that among the
Bantu religion provides a powerful sanction for the chieftainship.

When a man dies there is a long series of ritual acts to be
carried out before the dead man is finally 'brought back home'
as an ancestor. Following on the various rites of mourning there
comes, after from three to nine months or so, the 'bringing
home', as the Zulu put it, of the *itongo* or spirit: in essence the
ceremony consists of the first sacrifice to the dead man (as an
ancestor). Previous to this he had made known his presence either
in the form of a snake or lizard basking in the sun near the grave
or visiting the cattle kraal or the huts, or he has appeared to his
relatives in a dream. Should he have done none of these things foul
play is suspected, and a magician is summoned to call him home.

Day in, day out, the ancestors take part in the lives of the
people. No beer-drinking is held but they receive their libation;
no feast is held but they receive their portion. But there are certain occasions in the life of the family and of the tribe when the
ancestors must be specially assembled and propitiated, and these
are the occasions of sacrifice.

Connected with ancestor worship is the sacred fire which is
found in the Western tribes. Among the Herero each family
group has its own kraal. On the eastern side of the kraal is the hut
of the chief wife of the headman, and in front of this is the altar,
okuruo, on which burns perpetually the sacred fire of the
ancestors. This fire is guarded day and night by the chief wife of
the headman or by her daughters. At night it is taken into the hut,
and each morning it is carried out again to the altar. There, by the

fire, the oxen are killed for sacrificial feasts, and their skulls lie around it and are used as seats for the men of the kraal, while near by is the small *umumborombonga* tree, i.e. the sacred fig-tree, or a dry branch of the *omuvapu* ('roseintje') bush, which can be used if no fig-tree can be made to grow. The fig-tree is the symbol of the ancestors, and in the north of the Herero country there is a great fig-tree which is though of as the seat of all the ancestors, and so is regarded as most sacred.

Besides the ancestral spirits the Southern Bantu also believe in a universal deity who never was human. While the conception of this universal spirit differs from people to people there is little doubt that most of the tribes think of it more as a power manifest-ing itself in natural phenomena than as a god, though personal attributes are often given to it. This power shows itself more impressively in the phenomena of the weather: rain, thunder, lightning, are all considered as its manifestations. Among the Tsonga there is a very impersonal conception of this power, and Tilo, 'Heaven', is thought of as presiding over all unaccountable and inevitable phenomena of the atmosphere, of the fields, and of human existence. Sometimes Tilo is addressed as Hosi, 'Lord'. Here as it seems is a power scarcely personal, which is partly creative, partly a personification of the weather, partly a great power working in the universe.

Among the Zulu these conceptions have crystallized, and we find a Creator God, Unkulunkulu, 'the great, great one', and a Weather God, Inkosi, 'chief', who resembles in many respects Tilo of the Tsonga. According to the Zulu legends, mankind came out of a bed of reeds (Nhlanga). Now Unkulunkulu is said to be he who 'broke off the nations' from Nhlanga; he is thus the creator of man, and he also made the sun and moon, etc. As the Zulu put it, 'All things were made by the first man Unkulunkulu, they were made by him.' At the same time he is the great, great ancestor of the people, but his 'house' is not represented on earth today—he is prior to all peoples. Yet although Unkulunkulu had far greater powers than the ancestors of living men he is not to be compared with the Hebrew or Christian conception of the Creator. He is the great, wonderful, first man, but he is not wor-shipped, for he has no intimate representatives on earth. Inkosi (iZulu), on the other hand, is in the firmament, and he it is who brings all the storms and natural happenings. Certain men are beloved of iZulu or Inkosi—they can control Heaven provided they lead a life of strict ritual purity, and Heaven, too, will revenge any harm to them. Similar conceptions are apparently held of Modimo by the Central tribes, and of Kalunga (Ambo) or Ndjambi Karunga (Herero) by the Western tribes.

Politically the area of the Western Bantu (p. 119) comprehends the Cameroons, Rio Muni (Spanish), Gabon, Congo (Brazzaville) and Congo (Léopoldville), Angola (Portuguese), and Rhodesia, with a fraction of Mozambique north of the Zambezi. In this vast area lies the true 'Heart of Africa', the tropical rainforest of the Congo, the home of such little-known beasts as the okapi and of pygmy hunting tribes, but it equally includes, or included, the territory of considerable and highly organized kingdoms, such as the medieval kingdoms of the Kongo and the Lunda, and in later times the Bushongo Empire. Johnston, in his great work on the Bantu languages, enumerated over 150 tribes in this area speaking Bantu or semi-Bantu tongues. Here it is possible to do no more than refer to a few groupings of special importance or historical interest.

Ethnically the Northern fringe of the Southern Bantu merges gradually into the Central tribes of the Western Bantu, as in the case of the Lozi, who speak the language of their former Southern overlords. The Chokwe (Kioko) of Angola and the Congo have also some Southern affinities, while the Ila reached their present habitat from each of Nyasa. To the north of these and kindred tribes we find the solid mass of Luba-Lunda tribes, extending, roughly speaking, between Tanzania and Malawi in the east to Kasai in the west. To these belong the Bemba, Bisa, Aushi, Shila, and the Luluwa, Songe, and Luba-Hemba. To the north of the Sankuru River and part of the Kasai is the medley of tribes called Songo-Meno, which is transitional between the Luba-Bemba group and the Mongo tribes who dwell north of the 4th parallel of southern latitude. East of the Luange River is the domain of the Wongo-Lele-Bushongo congeries, specially known for their skill in wood-carving. As already stated, the southern limit of the

Western Bantu is vague; the formation of the Lunda Empire, the Yaka raids, and the subsequent encroachments of the Chokwe (Kioko) have played havoc with tribal organization. The Teke (Anziques, Angica, and many variants) occupy a vast region on the right bank of the Congo north of Stanley Pool, extending far inland; further north, Gabon, as far as the upper reaches of the Ogowe, is now largely peopled by the Pangwe (Fang, p. 136), who have led a roving existence and in their various expeditions and temporary conquests have left their indelible mark on most tribes north of the Ogowe, among whom racial purity scarcely exists until in the Cameroons we reach the northern limit of the Bantu and 'Sudanic' influences make themselves felt.

Of the old kingdom of the Kongo we get some idea from the early explorers. When in 1484, at the instance of Prince Henry the Navigator, Diego Çao discovered the Congo, the chiefs, from the sea to the river Kwango, from the Cuanza to the Kwilu, were under the jurisdiction of one king. Knivet's narrative preserves for us a record of the state maintained by the sovereign at the end of the sixteenth century:

The King of Congo, when hee goeth to the Campe to see his Armie, rideth an Elephant in great pompe and majestie, on either side of the Elephant he hath six slaves two of them were Kings, that he himselfe had taken in the field; all the rest were of noble birth; some of them were brothers to the King of Ancica [the land of the Bateke near Stanley Pool] and some of them were of the chiefest bloud of the great King of Bengala [Imbangala, another name for, or a branch of, the Jaga]. . . . Then there followeth a More, which doth nothing but talke aloud in praise of the King, telling what a great Warriour he hath beene, and praising his wisdome for all things that hee hath accomplished. . . .

Allowing for exaggeration in the early accounts—and we may question the accuracy of Knivet's statement that the elephant had been domesticated—it is certain that there was once a great and important kingdom of the Kongo. Moreover, other empires, such as those of the Lunda, arose, had their day, and disappeared, so that in this area there is a practical contrast to the relatively permanent kingdoms of the Guinea Coast. In the light of our present knowledge we have no warrant for saying that this is due to the infusion of Hamitic blood, rather may we look to the influence of environment and in the case of the kingdom of the Kongo the early and vehement introduction of Christianity. The population —as it seems—was largely composed of peoples living in independent, unconsolidated, and usually small groups, subject to no central government. For a time the superior military strength of migrant tribes permitted a political control to be established, but always environment, and perhaps a definite repugnance to this form of government, resulted in a more or less rapid disintegration. Often the origin of a state is to be traced to a stranger of outstanding ability; thus the Lunda Empire tradition-ally originated in a Luba hunter from the north-east, who with a band of followers settled among the far more numerous Lunda whose home is the highlands constituting eastern Angola and the south-west portion of the Congo. This empire, which flourished in the eighteenth and the early nineteenth century, extended from the river Kwango to the Lualaba, and is not only interesting from the point of view of history but important even nowadays as accounting for the present-day distribution of territory. The son of the founder of the Lunda Empire (by a Lunda woman of chiefly rank) was the father of Yamvo, and Mwata Yamvo became the hereditary title of the Lunda emperors. These continually added to their power by sending out relatives to form tributary king-doms, and in this manner arose the states of Kazembe on the east and of Mai Munene on the north. Another kingdom, that of Kasongo, further north on the River Lualaba, was also an off-shoot of the Lunda Empire, whose parent stock, the Luba, divided into a large number of tribes, have spread across the continent as far as the Kasai, being themselves known in the east as the Bashilange. The Songe are an important section of the Luba, north of whom are the Tetela.

In the Kasai region is an important group of peoples known by their neighbours as the Kuba. The dominant tribe of the group is the Mbala, who call themselves Bushongo, 'people of the throw-ing knife'. The origin of these people is uncertain, but it would seem that the Mbala at least have close links with some of the Mongo tribes to the north of the Sankuru River. The Mbala subdued the other Kuba tribes, and established an empire which was still important when they were studied by Torday in 1907–8. Moreover we may reasonably regard their politico-social organization as to some extent reflecting that of the old kingdom of the Kongo.

As the result of these and other invasions the Bantu of the Congo can be regarded as forming three groups: a western, comprising the people of the Lower Congo and Lower Kasai; a southern, comprising those of the Upper Kasai and Sankuru and of Katanga; and a third, the Mongo peoples to the north, inhabiting the Congo Basin proper.

As to the physical characters of the Bantu of the Congo, it is obvious that in so huge an area there must be variation. Generally speaking, the head is long, the nose broad and often flat, there is usually considerable prognathism, and the lips are thick; as usual among Negroids the legs are thin. Yet among such tribes as the Tetela there is a definitely round-headed element. Again, almost everywhere individuals are described of a type less frankly Negro than their fellows; such have thinner lips, higher and less broad noses, more hair on the face, and often a lighter skin colour, but since both types are said to occur in the same tribe and even in the same village no classificatory value can be attached to them in the present stage of our knowledge.

The following measurements add some degree of precision to these very general statements. The Fiote or Fjort of the Lower Congo, i.e. of the area which was the cultural centre of the old kingdom of the Kongo, are dolichocephalic with an average stature of about 66 inches. The Kongo, to the south of the river in the cataract region extending to Stanley Pool, have a cephalic index of 74 and a stature of 65 inches. The Ngala, about the bend of the middle river, are rather more dolichocephalic and slightly taller. The Soko of the Congo-Aruwimi confluence are shorter, averaging 63¾ inches, and verge upon and perhaps reach brachycephaly, with a cephalic index of slightly over 80. All these tribes are of the Congo proper. Coming to its tributaries, the Luba of the Kasai and Sankuru Rivers are high mesocephals, almost attaining to brachycephaly, with a stature of 66½ inches and 65¾ inches respectively; the Tetela of the Lubefu give an average cephalic index of 78 on the skull, equivalent to one of about 80 on the living, the five highest measurements giving figures from 81 to 84, while of the whole series 9 out of 50 (male) and 2 out of 27 (female) give an index of 80 or over.

Socially the highest development of the Western Bantu is found among the Bushongo (between the Sankuru and Lulua Rivers), who have a highly organized system of government, consisting of a hierarchy of ministers presided over by the king (*nyimi*). The ministry is composed of the prime minister (*kimi kambu*), the minister of war (*nyibita*), the four representatives of the provinces into which the kingdom is divided, and two women, daughters of former kings. One of these women is the more important, and in times of peace wears a bowstring round her neck which, on the outbreak of war, she hands solemnly to the *nyibita*, the final decision of war or peace resting with her. Below these dignitaries come descending grades of innumerable court officials, and representatives of trades, guilds, and sub-tribes (including pygmies). An important person is the official historian, who must be the son of a king and who takes precedence over the other princes, his duty being the preservation of ancient legend and history. At the meetings of the Great Council the king sits on a dais surrounded by his six male and two female ministers, and next to him, on a higher seat, is his mother, whose position is considered even more exalted than his. Many of the officials have judicial functions, and in addition there are twelve judges. In theory it is the king who nominates his councillors, but in reality he has little say in the matter; a guild will itself decide on its representative, and in all other appointments public opinion carries the day, sometimes in opposition to the king's expressed wishes.

The temporal power of the king is indeed strictly limited, and over such sub-tribes as the Ngongo and the Ngendi he has mainly a spiritual ascendancy. To his own people, the Mbala, he is both political chief and religious head. He is the living link joining them, through his predecessors, to Bumba the founder, and as such he is indeed Chembe Kunji, 'God on Earth'. In each king is incarnated the spirit of Bumba, who makes the sun shine, sends the rain to refresh the earth after a drought, and is responsible for the fertility of all living things. Any insult to the king is an insult to the whole clan, and any weakening of his power a danger to the community; in fact, among his own people his position is comparable with that of the Shilluk king (pp. 114–15). Formerly he was never allowed to touch the ground, but was carried on men's shoulders, and when he sat down it was on the back of a slave.

The lineage of the king is traced through one hundred and twenty predecessors, and part of the coronation ceremony is the recitation by the king-elect of all these ancestral names. The earlier are naturally mythological rather than historical, but one of these rulers, Shamba Bolongongo—the national hero of the Bushongo, to whom every possible wonder is attributed and whose sayings are continuously quoted—seems to have been a really remarkable person. He reorganized the system of government, encouraged the arts and crafts, and sought to abolish war by forbidding the use of the bow and arrow and of the *shongo* (throwing-knife), until then the national weapon of the Bushongo; while to his reign is attributed the importation of tobacco, the invention of the use of palm-oil, the introduction of the art of embroidery—at which the Bushongo now excel all other African peoples—and the growing of cassava.

The north-western limit of the Bantu is reached in the Cameroons, where (besides the pygmy) we have to deal with the Sudanic-speaking Negro. In general the Bantu occupy the forest belt and the Sudanic Negroes the grassland and mountain areas, but mention should be made of a number of tribes along the line of junction, said to present especially mixed racial characters and commonly described as speaking languages called semi-Bantu.

There does not seem to be any general difference in the physical characters of the Bantu- and the Sudanic-speaking tribes of the Cameroons. Their stature is about the same, while to the presence of round-headed pygmies in this area may presumably be ascribed the general tendency to brachycephaly. What difference there is in head-form is more fairly expressed in percentages than in averages in this very mixed area, or, in general terms, while both groups are predominantly mesocephalic the Bantu group tends to dolichocephaly and the Sudanic to brachycephaly.

The Bantu-speaking Pangwe (not to be confused with the Mpongwe, a settled Bantu people of Gabon), Oshyeba, etc., a group of tribes collectively known as Fang, appear to have originated somewhere west of the Congo-Nile divide and to have raided across Africa to the west coast. They are now the most important people of Gabon, occupying most of the country between the southern boundary of Spanish Guinea and the Ogowe River. They have attained considerable celebrity as cannibals, and it was of them—no doubt with some exaggeration—that Mary Kingsley wrote:

He does it [cannibalism] in his common-sense way. He will eat his next-door neighbour's relations and sell his own deceased to his next-door neighbour in return; but he does not buy slaves and fatten them up ... as some of the Middle Congo tribes do. ... He has no slaves, no prisoners of war, no cemeteries.

Physically the Fang are moderately tall men, with an average stature of 66½ inches. They are high mesocephals, if not actually brachycephalic, and when first mentioned by Bowdich more than a hundred years ago were described by him as an inland people with such relatively refined features that he considered them allied to the Fulani, i.e. we should now recognize in them a pronounced Hamitic strain. No doubt miscegenation has gone on at an increased rate during the last century, but even at the present time they are described as well-built, tall, and slim, with a brown complexion often inclined to yellow, well-developed beard, and a projecting forehead. Part of their reputation for ferocity may, perhaps, be attributed to their systematic filing of their incisors, and sometimes their canine teeth, to a point.

9
Bantu (*continued*)

Of the Eastern Bantu (delimited on p. 118) the tribes—they might almost be called nations—grouped round the shores of Lake Victoria and Lake Albert possess so many characters in common that they are well brought together under the single term interlacustrine Bantu (Group Ia, p. 119). For a considerable time, perhaps some hundreds of years, they have existed as a number of kingdoms, the best known being Buganda, Bunyoro, and Karagwe, but their history indicates that at one time they all formed part of a greater unit, the Kituara Empire. Other 'interlacustrine' tribes are the Rwanda, east of Lake Kivu; Rundi, north of Lake Tanganyika; Sukuma, in Usukuma, south of Lake Victoria; the Luyia or Bantu Kavirondo, east of Lake Victoria; Haya, west of Lake Victoria; and Nyamwezi, in Unyamwezi, east of Lake Tanganyika. It seems that all these tribes have a Hamitic (presumably Galla) element, brought in by the Huma, far more recent than those incoming waves of Hamitic blood which, mixing with the Negro, originally gave rise to the Bantu.

To return to the Kituara Empire. As is but natural each of its peoples tells the story to its own glorification, but the Buganda story is that their common founder and first ruler, Kintu, came from the north bringing with him a single cow, goat, chicken, banana root, and sweet potato, which, increasing miraculously, soon stocked the country, the potato being especially apportioned to Bunyoro and the banana to Buganda. Presently Kintu became weary of his people's stupidities and bloodsheddings and disappeared, but since it was known that he did not die it became traditional for his successors to seek for him. At last he was found by a king, Ma'anda, as an aged man seated on a throne in the forest, his beard white with age and his followers white-skinned as the white man and clothed in white robes. The story tells how Ma'anda committed an act of bloodshed, whereupon Kintu and his followers vanished and have been seen no more. Here is a fairly definite account indicating the advent from the north of a 'white', i.e. Hamitic, aristocracy, and another version with less mythical elaboration was recorded by Emin Pasha. No doubt it is at least in part due to this 'European' influence that we find the curious mixture of primitive and advanced elements in the social institutions of the interlacustrine communities. Thus, among the Ganda we have, on the one hand, the horrible slaughter that occurred after the death of a king, on the other hand the advanced organization of the state, with, at its head, the king (*kabaka*), with his *lukiko* or council, of which the chief members were the *katikiro* (prime minister and chief justice), the *kimbugwe*, who had charge of the king's umbilical cord, and a high chief from each of the main districts into which the country was divided. Each chief accounted for his people to the *katikiro* and thus through him to the king.

Among the Nyoro the invaders from the north have fused less completely with the older inhabitants than in the case of the Ganda, so that two classes remained distinct in the body politic— the pastoral Huma, and the Iru, the original agriculturists and artisans, whom the Huma regard more or less as serfs. Later there is said to have arisen a third group originating among the Iru and so far accepted by the pastoral class that they were allowed to intermarry with the daughters of the latter. It has been claimed that the totemic system reflects this triple organization, since three classes of totems can be recognized: those relating to cattle alone, others connected with both cattle and plants, and a third class with plants only. It is however, probable that this scheme presents a somewhat artificial simplification of the problem.

Among the Nyankole assimilation between the two stocks has not gone nearly so far as among the Ganda or even the Nyoro (pp. 101–2). It might indeed be said that assimilation has scarcely gone beyond the possession of a common language spoken both by the intruding Huma and the indigenous Iru. The Huma are cow people, owning large herds if they are rich, or acting as herdsmen if they are poor; the Iru, on the other hand, were rarely allowed to possess cattle and had to provide grain and beer for the Huma.

Physically the Ganda are described as showing a wide range of variation. This probably applies especially to skin colour, type of nose, and thickness of lips, all characters that would readily vary according to the amount of Hamitic and Negro blood in the clan or family, for with regard to stature and head-form the statement is hardly borne out by the considerable number of measurements published. The Ganda may be taken to be rather stoutly-built men of medium height, averaging about $65\frac{1}{4}$ inches, with a mean cephalic index (according to Roscoe and Oschinsky) of 73. The men have a scrupulous regard for decency, carried to such an extent that in the time of King Mutesa a heavy fine was inflicted on courtiers who exposed their legs to view in the king's presence. Moreover, they have shown a desire for education and a readiness to adopt the white man's civilization and religion. The house of the better-class Muganda is very superior to the ordinary African hut: the lofty high-pitched roof is supported by slender columns of palm and covered with a thick thatch neatly shaved to a smooth edge, while the appearance of the interior of the hut as well as the porch and veranda is enhanced by a canework of elephant grass, a speciality of the Ganda.

Among the interlacustrine Bantu the royal residence, it might almost be called palace, constitutes a large and elaborate series of buildings within an enclosure and includes those housing the sacred royal drums, to which, at least among the Nyankole, offerings of beer and milk are made. Many of these people maintain a sacred herd, set aside for the use of the king, the milk of which he drinks with the utmost ceremony. In Buganda the cult of the numerous deities was under the immediate control of the king, while the ghosts of kings were placed on an equality with the gods and received the same honour and worship. The death of a king was formerly accompanied by much bloodshed, a Nyoro king being buried in a grave lined with the living bodies of his wives and retainers, whose arms and legs had previously been

F

broken to prevent their escape. The death of a Ganda king was announced by the extinction of the sacred fire which burned near the entrance of the royal enclosure and the strangling of the chief who had charge of it. The king's body, after special treatment, was buried with many victims; five months later the jawbone was taken from the skull and placed beside the umbilical cord (carefully preserved during lifetime) in a temple specially built for it, where it was thenceforth guarded by the ex-queen. Among the Nyankole a commoner is buried in the dung-heap, but the body of a king is taken to the royal burial-place in the Ensanzi forest, where some days later the priest of the temple produces a lion-cub and presents it to the people as the spirit of the dead king. The king's body is then buried with little ceremony, and the cub is carefully reared, being later released to join its fellows, believed to be spirits of former kings and therefore sacred, though lions in other parts of the kingdom may be killed with impunity.

Apart from the interlacustrine Bantu the Eastern Bantu fall into two great divisions, a North-Eastern and a true Eastern (p. 119).

The North-Eastern tribes (group I*b*) of the Eastern Bantu include the Pokomo of Tana River Valley, the Nyika, the Kamba between Tana River and Mt. Kilimanjaro, the Kikuyu round Mt. Kenya, the Taita in the Taita hills, and the Chaga on the southern slopes of Kilimanjaro. Of these tribes the Kamba and Kikuyu are probably the most important; they are certainly the best known, and like the remainder of the group have been considerably affected in culture by the Masai and other Nilo-Hamitic peoples.

South of these tribes the remaining—true Eastern Bantu—group (I*c*) fall into two great sub-groups, viz. (1) East Coast Bantu, in Tanzania and Mozambique, and (2) East Central or Nyasa Bantu in Zambia and round Lake Nyasa. The former includes the Sambara and Sagara of north-east Tanzania; the Sango, Gogo, and Hehe of central and southern Tanzania; the coastal Swahili; the Konde, between the Rufiji and Ruvuma Rivers; and the Makua, from north of the Ruvuma River to the northern half of the Zambezi delta. The East Central section includes the Ngonde, the Nyakyusa, and their neighbours, north and north-east of Lake Nyasa; the Fipa, on the southern shores of

Lake Tanganyika; the Nyanja (including Nsenga, Sena, Chewa), south and south-west of Lake Nyasa down to the Zambezi River; and the Yao, between the Ruvuma and Lujenda Rivers east of Lake Nyasa, who link up again with the Makua. It is worth noting that a number of these tribes belong in great part to the earlier Bantu migrations, and that reflex movements northwards had produced disorder long before Arab raids and Ngoni incursions spread ruin and desolation.

The Nyika (*supra*, I*b*), so called from the Swahili word meaning 'forest and thorn bush country', are a group of tribes who, during the sixteenth century, under pressure from the Galla, migrated down the coast from the poor country on the left bank of the Tana River. The term is not however used indiscriminately, and does not include such peoples as the Pokomo, though they are ethnically connected with the tribes to whom it is applied. The Giryama, now living about 3° south of the Equator, are probably the most important of the group, whose members are, generally speaking, tall, muscular, well set up, and long-headed. Waist-cloths are worn by the men, and women wear many-pleated kilts, but are nude from the waist up, though now the tendency is to dress like Swahili women.

The Nyika tribes are divided into exogamous clans which observe certain prohibitions and avoidances and share a general veneration for the hyena, in which all the cognate tribes join except the Pokomo. Every clan has its own club-house, and there is also a council-house, which is the general inter-clan meeting-place for men and houses the friction drum used for convening the council. The Nyika are essentially agricultural, with many sheep and goats but few cattle. Some, if not all the tribes, carry swords, which are, however, as much implements as weapons, while the Giryama have a parrying-stick, said to be unique in this area.

The Nyika worship the widespread Eastern Bantu deity, Mulungu, who, in one aspect at least, is the Dispenser and Creator from whose union with the earth have sprung all things in the world, including human beings, who are the hens and chickens of Mulungu.

The Kamba, one of the largest tribes in East Africa, occupy part of the eastern slope of the East African highlands between the upper course of the River Tana and the Uganda railway. Their neighbours in the west and north-west are the Kikuyu, and to the south are the Nilo-Hamitic Masai, their inveterate enemies. The Kamba are high dolichocephals (C.I. over 76), with an average stature of about 64 inches. They are divided into a number of totemic clans, most of which seem to be named after the ancestor, but may also be referred to by the name of the totem. As so often happens the members of a clan are supposed to possess the characteristics of the totem animal: thus the members of the lion clan are courageous and spirited, those of the hyena clan characterized by perpetual greed. Properly speaking, there are no chiefs; government is in the hands of a council of elders, of a purely local character and with no authority for the whole country, though occasionally a rich man with a commanding personality has attained to the leadership of an extensive territory. The council has judicial and religious functions, decides questions of war (i.e. raids), and its members officiate at sacrifices; for warfare temporary leaders were selected.

The Kamba have age-sets, and within them rank-classes. The position of a man within his set is marked by the part that he may eat of the goats paid as fees to the set. Except for the sets carrying the privilege of sitting on the council, a dignity usually reached between the ages of 40 and 50, a man may belong to any set on payment of the proper fees.

The medicine man's functions include prophecy, divination, and the curing of sickness, and he is consulted on all the perplexing occasions of life. With the elders he is guardian of the ancestral cult, and he tells the elders when to sacrifice to the spirits and gives instructions for carrying out the rites.

Formerly the Kamba men went naked, but nowadays European blankets are worn by both sexes. Cicatrization is practised, mostly by the women, and both sexes chip a number of the front teeth of the upper jaw into points, in addition to removing two lower incisors; as a result of this custom the teeth tend to break off above the gum, when 'false' teeth made of the bone of goat or hartebeest may be pegged into the roots. The bow and

poisoned arrow and a dagger are the usual weapons; they have
never used spears and shields.

The Kamba are chiefly agriculturists; the cultivation is carried
on almost exclusively by the women, with hoe and digging-stick;
and no instruments of iron are permitted lest the rain should no
longer fall. Cattle, sheep, and goats are kept, and though the
cattle are herded by boys and men the milking is done by women.
Like the Masai and Kikuyu, the Kamba occasionally bleed their
cattle, blood being a favourite food: a ligature is fastened tightly
round the animal's neck, causing a swelling of the great vein, at
which a stopped arrow is shot, and the blood is caught in a
calabash and drunk or made into soup with milk or millet flour.

The Creator and Supreme Being, Mulungu, dwells in the sky
and is seldom worshipped. 'Mulungu does us no evil, so where-
fore should we sacrifice to him?' is the characteristic attitude, but
in every Kamba family offerings are made to the ancestral spirits
at every meal, in addition to the public cult superintended by the
elders.

In some districts the dead are not buried, but are dragged out
into the bush and left for the hyenas. After a death no one may
have sexual intercourse until the village has been purified; the
elder performing the rite sacrifices a goat and sprinkles the
stomach contents over the assembled mourners and on the walls
and the bed in the hut where the death took place. Before the
process of purification is completed the widow must sleep with
the dead man's brother or successor as her husband; if there are
several widows only the 'big' wife need undergo this ceremony.

The Kikuyu inhabit the highlands of Kenya, where they say
that they superseded a race of hunters (perhaps the predecessors
of the present Dorobo) and a diminutive race known as the
Agumba, now extinct. The Kikuyu attribute their own origin to
the Kamba, their neighbours to the south-east—with closely
similar language and customs—from whom they differ little in
physique (C.I. 76, stature about $64\frac{1}{2}$ inches).

The Kikuyu are divided into exogamous patrilineal clans,
connected by blood ties, but not restricted to any particular area.
Some clans have a recognized headman, others have not, but each
has its hereditary taboos and traditions: thus the Gachiku clan

must not work iron or act as circumcisors, and the males of the M'wesaga clan are able to see rain coming and to stop it. A man's rank in the tribe depends on his relation to the rising generation, and the first step is reached when he becomes the father of a child; he then enters a body called *moranja*. When his first child is initiated he joins the *kiama kia athamaki*, the elders who arbitrate cases, and later advances to the grade of *maturanguru* elders, who sacrifice to God on behalf of the community and wear a particular type of ear-ring.

The Kikuyu country is extremely fertile, though badly eroded in many areas, and the people are essentially agriculturists. The principal crop is maize, others being pigeon pea, potatoes, manioc, bananas, sugar-cane, and yams. Cattle are regarded as the embodiment of wealth and are the valued property of the few, but the goat is taken as the unit of value, and for a wife a man pays so many 'goats', though the actual payment may take the form of cattle, sheep, and goats, the ratio of value of goats to cattle being as 13 to 1. The cattle are grazed on the edge of the cultivation and herded at night in well-guarded enclosures; everything connected with them is done by men and boys. Every wife has her quota of sheep and goats, which at night are kept in the owner's hut.

The word for the Deity, N'gai, is of Masai origin. His dwelling is localized in different places, but especially on Mt. Kenya and in sacred trees (known as *mugumu*, generally a species of ficus), where sacrifice is offered by the elders. N'gai hears and answers prayer, but the ills of life are attributed to departed spirits, and the medicine man is called in to interpret their desires. In addition to the 'orthodox religion' there exists a semi-secret snake cult. The medicine man plays an important part in society, his services being particularly necessary for purification after ceremonial defilement (*thahu*) caused, e.g. by stepping over or touching a corpse, digging a grave, eating forbidden food, etc.

A corpse is either thrown out on to uncultivated land or left in the hut for the hyenas to drag away. Burial is reserved for the old and rich, when the grave is dug by the sons of the deceased outside the door of the hut; the body is buried lying on its side with the head to the west, knees drawn up, and head resting on the palm of the right hand if a man, of the left if a woman. The hut is then pulled down on top of the grave.

One of the most mysterious of Kikuyu rites is the symbolic second birth, undergone by both sexes at the age of about 10, and consisting of a dramatization of the birth of the child. Until the new birth has been undergone no individual can be circumcised, inherit property, or take part in the religious rites of the country. If the mother is not living, another woman acts in her place, and in future is looked upon as the mother of the child, and similarly an elder may act as proxy in the place of the father.

The Chaga, inhabiting the slopes of Kilimanjaro, are a people of composite origin with numerous clans, the majority tracing their descent to a founder of Kamba or Taita stock. They appear to be comparatively recent immigrants, i.e. within the last few hundred years. They are essentially agricultural, with a skilful system of artificial irrigation. Villages do not exist, but each man's homestead is situated in the midst of his banana grove, making a continuous plantation of bananas intersected by hedges of *dracaena*. Chiefship is hereditary, the succession normally passing to the eldest son of the senior wife, and the mother of the chief is treated with the greatest respect. The chief's power is believed to have formerly been of a despotic nature, though there was, on the whole, little pomp attached to his surroundings, nor was he distinguished by any insignia or symbol of his dignity.

Two types of huts are in use, one conical in shape, and the other a comparatively low hut with slightly curved roof suggesting Masai origin. About half the interior is occupied by a cattle stall, for the Chaga have many cattle, and owing to the scarcity of grazing (the country being thickly inhabited and largely cultivated) over half the stock is kept stalled in the owner's huts and fed on grass cut and carried from the valley—a work involving much labour. The people are clever workers in wood, and their smiths are skilful and supply ironwork largely to the Masai; the smith's craft is known to certain clans only, but there are no restrictions on intermarriage.

'Circumcision' of both sexes is practised and there are elaborate initiation ceremonies. The boys may be circumcised only when a son of the chief arrives at the proper age; then there is a general circumcision, after which the youths form or join a group called a *rika* to which a specific name is given. The institution is derived from the Masai, and establishes a new warrior class. After initiation a girl is shut up in a cage in her mother's hut for three months, fed on fattening food and daily anointed; at the end of this period she is considered fit for marriage.

At death the corpse is doubled up with the head and legs tied together 'to resemble a small barrel'. Having been anointed with fat and red ochre it is covered with the hide of a sacrificed bull and placed in the grave in a sitting posture facing the Kibo peak of Kilimanjaro. A man is buried within the hut of his senior wife. About eighteen months after death the bones are exhumed and placed in the banana grove, the skull being taken to the ancestral grove or, in some instances, deposited in an earthen jar. Chiefs are not buried in a hide but in a hollow section of a tree-trunk, plugged at the ends, and their death may be kept secret for as long as two years. Formerly, childless and unmarried persons and children were not buried but left in the bush for the hyenas.

The Chaga name for the supreme being is Ruwa, also the word for the sun. Ruwa now pays little attention to mankind (though he liberated the first human beings from the vessel imprisoning them), and Chaga religion is essentially the cult of ancestral spirits, back to the 'forgotten ones' who, receiving no sacrifices, gradually disappear. To ancient spirits no sacrifices are offered unless they be founders of clans: 'the Lord of the Land', the first to settle in the land. The ancestry is divided into those of the right and those of the left: the spirits of the right-hand side are the more powerful, and their leader is the paternal grandfather, while on the left-hand side the principal spirit is that of the maternal grandfather. Any general calamity is attributed to the anger of the chief's ancestors or to the spirits of the conquered chiefs from whom the country was taken, and these must likewise be appeased.

Of the true Eastern (*supra*, Ic) division of the Eastern Bantu the Swahili are especially important, since the language they speak has become the lingua franca of a great part of eastern Africa, extending from the western Congo eastwards past the great lakes and out into the ocean to include the Comoro Islands off the north-western coast of Madagascar. The Lamu archipelago is generally acknowledged as the cradle of the tribe, but their territory now extends over a long stretch of the coastal belt—from the Equator to about 16° S.—including Zanzibar and Pemba. They speak a language said to be specially closely akin to Giryama, but it certainly contains many Arabic words and a sprinkling from other languages, including Somali, Portuguese, and Galla, the whole modified by local influences so that at the present day there are a considerable number of dialects. It would then be surprising if it were possible to define the physical characters of the Swahili: an Arab, or at least a man speaking good Arabic, able to read the Koran, and with a mind attuned to Arabic civilization, will call himself a Swahili; so will a 'black' with Negro features, a flat nose, spiralled hair, the descendant, maybe, of a slave mother and an unknown father. The people are then a mixture of mixtures, the African elements having been influenced from the seventh century onwards by a succession of waves from Persia and from the Arabic east. Nor in estimating the physical make-up of the Swahili must it be forgotten that Zanzibar was for many years the greatest slave mart of East Africa.

The Yao believe themselves to be descended from the same stock as the Nyanja; they originally seem to have inhabited the mountains between Lake Nyasa and the Mozambique coast, whence they spread towards the Shire Highlands. Here, in course of time, they settled down side by side with the local population and have intermarried to some extent with the Nyanja. They are described as a sturdy people, stronger than the Nyanja, with a good proportion of tall men, and were much in request as carriers. They are divided into matrilineal clans, each with its own distinctive name.

The Yao chip the edge of the upper incisors into saw-like points and scar their temples. There are initiation ceremonies for both sexes. Marriage is matrilocal, and, as among the Nyanja, the bridegroom, having obtained the consent of the girl and of her relatives (above all of the maternal uncle), builds a house at the bride's home. After the marriage (which is ratified by porridge and a fowl eaten ceremonially by the parents of both parties) one of the first duties of the bridegroom is to hoe a garden for his mother-in-law. Ordinarily a man will have one or two free wives and perhaps four slaves; if he has more than one free wife he spends his time between their different villages, since each will remain at her home. He inherits the wives of his elder brother, and also of his maternal uncle if the latter has no younger brother living at the time of his death.

Like the Nyanja the Yao believe in a supreme being, Mulungu, who 'arranges the spirits of the dead in rows or tiers', and also in special deities of their own connected with the country whence they came, and therefore perhaps ancient chiefs. They also pay a certain amount of reverence to 'the old gods of the land', i.e. the spirits of dead Nyanja chiefs (and notably one Kangomba), who haunt the principal mountains whence they were driven in their lifetime by the Yao, and are specially appealed to for rain, so that a Nyanja who can trace connexion with Kangomba is often asked by the Yao chief to help him in his supplications. Every village has its 'prayer tree' under which sacrifices are offered. There is no priestly class, but religious functions are performed 'by a chief on behalf of the tribe, by the headman for the village, by the father for the family, and (in private matters) by the individual for himself'.

The Nyanja extend under several different names from the Shire Valley to the Luangwa and as far north as the middle of Lake Nyasa. At one time they appear to have been continuous in this region, but they have been displaced and broken up by the intrusions of strange tribes. Owing to blending with other tribes there is much variation in the physical character of the Nyanja, so that it is difficult to fix on a special type; they are described as of medium height, though tall individuals are fairly common, and one writer lays stress on their small jaws and weak mouths and chins. They have intermarried to some extent with the Yao. The descendants of the Kololo warriors stationed in the Lower Shire Valley by Livingstone have been absorbed into the surrounding Nyanja population, while the Nyanja west of the Upper Shire are subject to the Ngoni, with whom they are often confused. The Nyanja have from time immemorial been distinguished as iron-workers.

They believe in the existence of a supreme being, Mpambe or Mulungo, to whom they pray for rain; in some parts the word means 'thunder', and it is also applied to the spirits of the dead, who are propitiated with offerings placed in 'spirit huts' about two feet high, made of grass.

The dead are usually buried in groves or thickets, the corpse lying with the legs bent, and the house of the deceased is destroyed and the foundations dug over; but a chief is sometimes buried in his own house, which is then deserted.

10
Semites

BEFORE DISCUSSING THE ARABS OF AFRICA it will be necessary to define the meaning to be attached to the term as applied on this continent, and even to say something of its significance in their homeland, Arabia. The traditional Arab of the textbooks is long-headed, 'with a fine oval face ... [a] type which ... often assumes an almost ideal beauty'; yet a glance at literature shows at least as many brachycephals as dolichocephals, while anyone who has travelled in the Sudan knows that most of the Arabs he has met are dark-skinned, often frankly Negroid in features, sometimes practically black, with hair that may be almost Negro in quality. Additional difficulty has been caused by the indiscriminate use by the French of the word '*arabe*' for any Arabic-speaking African Muhammadan, a practice which, even if it does not add to the confusion in the Nile Valley, undoubtedly does so in Algeria and Morocco, where the majority of so-called Arabs of almost every French anthropologist, from the time of Broca onwards, present little or no evidence of Arab ancestry and must be regarded not as Arabs but as Berbers (Hamites), who, having adopted the Arabic language and Arab ideas, become more thoroughly arabized than their Berber-speaking countrymen. There still remains the contradiction between the dolichocephalic Arab of literature and the fact that there are round-headed 'Arabs' not only in Arabia but also in Libya, as shown by a number of skulls in the Museum at Florence. But a solution of the problem is suggested when it is remembered that an ancient Arab cemetery near Cairo has yielded a whole series of skulls which are hyperbrachycephalic, with a cephalic index of over 85, the explanation being that, besides the typical long-headed Arabs of Northern Arabia, the immigrants into the Nile Valley, and no doubt into Libya, included natives of the coast of Southern Arabia—an area of proved brachycephaly. In later times these Southerners formed part of the force invading Spain, where in their new home they and their descendants continued their old-time quarrels with their brethren of Northern Arabia.

It is then obvious that in Africa the term Arab may be applied to any people professing Islam, however much Negro or other foreign blood may run in their veins, so that while the term has a cultural value it is of little racial significance and often is frankly misleading. Yet, in a broad sense, and excluding the Berbers, the term remains of positive value as denoting a vast series of tribes, 'claiming, even if they have it not, a predominant Caucasian ["European"] ancestry, boasting a particular historic tradition and religion, and speaking a semitic language'. In this sense the peoples we call Arab contrast with all the other Africans we have discussed in that they exhibit an essentially uniform culture, even if in many instances they can boast but little of the newer immigrant blood to which this culture is attached.

At this stage it will be convenient to consider how the Arabs came to play the important part that they have in Africa. The conquest of Egypt by 'Amr ibn al-Ās in the years 639 to 641, important as were its results from the cultural aspect, cannot have had any great racial effect on the population of the Nile Valley. We know that the number of immigrant warriors was not great, and although villages still exist that are said to carry their history back to this, one of the first outpourings of Islam, it may be doubted whether this is much more than a tradition and an example of the constant tendency we meet with in the African to glorify the Asiatic, i.e. the Muhammadan, connexion. The great invasions of the eleventh century are on quite a different level; especially does this hold of the migration of the Beni Hillal (and kindred tribes) who in 1048 were launched by the Vizier of the Fatimid Caliph Mustansir against his master's more orthodox vassals in North Africa. Each man was provided with a camel and given a gold piece, the only condition being that he must settle in the west. In two years the invaders had pillaged Cyrenaica and Tripoli and had captured Kairouan, the Beni Hillal for the most part settling in Tripoli and Tunisia, while their companions pressed on westwards even into Morocco. This well exemplifies the process of arabization in North Africa, and it was to a large extent an eastern and southern reflux from the Hillalian invasion that had most to do with the arabization of the Nile Valley and is thus responsible for much of the present-day distribution of the Arab tribes of the Sudan. How this actually came about is most easily understood by quoting a passage from the great Arab historian, Ibn Khaldun:

At first the Kings of the Nuba attempted to repulse them, but they failed; then they won them over by giving them their daughters in marriage. Thus was their Kingdom disintegrated, and it passed to certain of the sons of the Guhayna on account of their mothers according to the custom of the infidels as to the succession of the sister or the sister's son. So their Kingdom fell to pieces and the A'rab of Guhayna took possession of it. But their rule showed none of the marks of statesmanship because of the inherent weakness of a system which is opposed to discipline and the subordination of one to another. Consequently they are still divided up into parties and there is no vestige of authority in their land, but they remain nomads following the rainfall like the A'rab of Arabia. There is no vestige of authority in their land since the result of the commingling and blending that has taken place has merely been to exchange the old ways for the ways of the Bedouin Arab.

At the present day the Arabs of Africa are best classified by the obvious common-sense criterion of their mode of life—whether sedentary or nomad—but it is worth remembering that going with this classification are the facts that the less mixed Arabs are found in the predominantly 'European' north and east, while in the south and west are those people who, although calling themselves Arabs, inhabit areas in which the Negro is or has been dominant, and thus carry much Negro blood. Accepting the sociological criterion, three main groups are to be distinguished:

(1) True nomads (Ahl Ibl, 'people of the camel').

(2) Baggara, cattle folk, nomad in a more restricted sense.

(3) Sedentaries, including (*a*) the Ahl Sawaki, 'the people of the Sakia', i.e. the riverain cultivators; and (*b*) other settled village folk.

Actually these three classes are not mutually exclusive. Some tribes, such as the Kenana of the Sudan, include all three, and many nomad tribes have sedentary sections, or there may even be a limited nomadism, as when a tribe sows its crops in an oasis in the autumn and leads a more or less wandering life until the spring. The distinction between camel-owners and cattle-owners is largely determined geographically, for camels are seldom taken south of 10° N. in the rains. The Baggara, in consequence of having been forced to live in the south, thus had to adopt cattle for transport instead of camels.

Tribal organization is far stronger among the nomads than among the sedentaries, who are generally looked down upon by the former unless they belong to a family regarded as particularly holy; they certainly are, as a rule, less pure-blooded than the wanderers. Each tribe is under the control of a head Sheikh, and among the nomads consists of a number of sections or divisions, called in the Sudan *khashm beit*, each with its own sheikh. Both offices tend to be hereditary, but are sometimes elective, and where the old tribal organization is still effective all the divisions acknowledge the ultimate authority of the head Sheikh, whose symbol of supreme authority is the *nahas*, the war drum of the tribe, with which is connected considerable ceremonial. Among the sedentary population, as already stated, tribal organization is much weaker, and though importance is still attached to the tribal pedigree a communal organization tends to take the place of the tribal.

It is among the nomads that the purest Arab physical type is found. Here in the rough wastes of north-west Kordofan are the two strongest and richest camel-owning tribes of the Sudan, the Kababish and the Kawahla, age-long rivals, who graze their herds over an area extending west to the Darfur border and south and east among such powerful, predominantly sedentary tribes as the Dar Hamid. Yet even here there is considerable variation, largely determined by the wealth of the tribe or tribal sections. Among the richer tribes there has been a steady infusion of Negro blood, proportionate as it seems to the wealth and therefore to the number of slaves found in the division. Thus it comes about that the Sheikh of the Kababish is remarkably dark-skinned—as indeed have been his ancestors for some generations—though in the case of the present ruler his features are far from Negroid [1930].

Until measurements of representative tribes of Sudan Arabs have been taken it is impossible to make any general statements as to physical characters, or as to what extent the purer tribes of African Arabs have kept their old physical qualities. In fact, the only data bearing on the subject are a small number of measurements of Kababish and of Aulad Ali. The latter people are of north-eastern Libya and are perhaps its strongest tribe; the measurements of the Kababish were taken among both the sedentary members of the tribe in Dongola and the nomads of Kordofan. All these measurements show a similarity amounting to identity, the more convincing as they were made by different observers who had no knowledge of each other's work:

	Stature	C.I.	N.I.
Aulad Ali (20)	67 in.	75·4	72·3
Kababish of Dongola (9) . .	67½ in.	74·5	68·8
Kababish of Kordofan (15) .	67 in.	74·1	70·2

It should be mentioned that both the Aulad Ali and the Kababish trace their origin to an old Arabian stock, the Beni 'Ukba.

Nothing definite can be said with regard to the physical characters of the sedentary Arabs; measurements do not exist, but so far as the Nile Valley north of Khartoum is concerned the opinion may be expressed that the majority of riverain tribes are darker-skinned and of a smaller, more slender build, than the nomad Arabs of the south and west.

In Egypt there are still a number of Arab groups sufficiently strong to maintain their old tribal names and organizations, i.e. true Arabs in blood and tradition. The more important of these include:

1. The Ma'aza of the Eastern Desert.
2. The Aulad Ali of the Behera district of the Delta, extending

across the frontier into Libya as the strongest nomadic tribe of the Tripolitan Desert.

3. The Harabi of the Faiyum, still true pastoral nomads and extending as such into the Tripolitan Desert.

4. The fisher-folk of Lake Menzaleh, who are said to trace their origin to Sinai.

5. The Howeitat of Matarieh, now practically sedentary.

All these tribes are dolichocephalic, with average indices ranging from about 73 to 75 and statures of 66 to 67 inches (with the exception of the Harabi, who are somewhat taller). Besides these properly organized peoples there are small groups of tent-dwelling gipsy-like folk, claiming to be Arabs, who wander about the edge of the cultivation in Upper Egypt, usually with a few starveling goats—a people dreaded and disliked by the fellahin, whom they victimize, in much the same way as gypsies are disliked in our own country.

The Baggara include a large number of tribes, primarily cattle-breeders and all nomadic within the limits required to provide water and pasture for their herds. Except where the tsetse fly is prevalent they roam over a large area in the southern Sudan, especially in southern Kordofan and Darfur, extending westwards as far as Lake Chad. Their bulls, which are well-trained and will carry from 200 to 300 lb., are their most valued possession, and it is on these that their women, children, and baggage are transported during migration. Racially, many of the Baggara tribes carry as much if not more Negro blood than Arab; the mixture has, however, produced some strikingly handsome individuals, who, although dark-skinned, often have clear-cut features, and especially well-formed noses. The Baggara are, perhaps, the most warlike of the Sudan Arabs, and formed the backbone of the army of the Khalifa, himself belonging to the Ta'aisha, a sub-tribe of the Habbania, which, with the Hawazma, Humr, and Messiria in Kordofan and the Rizeigat in Darfur, constitutes one of the most important of the tribes of the Baggara.

In Nigeria there are Arab colonies at Kano and at such trading centres as Sokoto, Zaria, etc., but much more important than these are the predominantly pastoral Arabs of Bornu, commonly known as Shuwa. Their ancestors, who claimed descent from the Prophet, are known to have been in Darfur and Wadai in the fifteenth century, and no doubt some of the present-day Arabs of these states are of the same stock; other offshoots have lost their identity and have become merged with such Nigerian peoples as the Kanuri. In the old days the Shuwa constituted the most important element in the Bornu army, and it was among them that whole troops of horsemen were protected by chain armour, said to date from the Crusades. Their language retains many classical words which have dropped out of the Arab dialects of more civilized Africa, and it is of interest that some of their technical terms are the same as those employed by the Kababish of the Bayuda steppe.

All the Arab tribes with which we have so far been concerned have been in the country probably for centuries, but there is one tribe of recent entry which should be mentioned. Occupying part of the eastern provinces of the Sudan are the Rasheida or Zebediye, noted for their breed of swift reddish-brown riding-camels. With a complexion of light wheaten colour their men are often strikingly handsome, while their good looks are not marred by the face scars with which so many of the Sudan Arabs disfigure their faces. Physically and socially they stand out as entirely un-African, and, indeed, their pedigrees record that the majority of their families have not been in the country for more than a few generations.

With the exception of the Baggara, who are easily inflamed, neither the Arabs of the Eastern nor Western Sudan have shown themselves fanatically Muhammadan, nor are they unduly super-stitious, the nomad in this respect contrasting strongly with the settled population of the Nile Valley. On the other hand, many of the nomads observe customs, e.g. those connected with the dead, which are certainly not Muhammadan and which, if they do not go back to the days of paganism in Arabia, definitely antedate Islam in Africa.

The religious confraternities of Islam, with their allied move-ments (such as the Mahdiya of the Sudan), have played and still play so large a part in the life of North Africa wherever there is any considerable Arab element that some account—however short—

must be attempted, it being realized that the geographical background is a waste and sterile land, with but scattered oases joined by routes so waterless that they can as a rule be traversed only by organized parties, a country propitious to a particular form of religious practice and politico-religious organization. Although most of the orders—named after their various founders—are based on Sufism, the mystical form of Islam, and at their inception were puritan and reformatory in purpose, they have generally before long become strongly political and practical in character, in the same way as did many monastic institutions in Christendom in medieval times. The constitution is much the same in all instances: there is a Sheikh or Imam with absolute authority as the direct representative of God and the Prophet, his authority being delegated to local heads. A strict novitiate is often required of adherents, though there are generally many lay members, and such membership need not interfere with ordinary life and work. The local centre, the *zawia* (properly a 'retreat' or 'hermitage'), may consist only of a mosque, but is often more extensive, including schools and houses for officials, and may be fortified. Naturally *zawia* are built at important halts on the caravan routes, where there is good water, and this enormously enhances their importance. Each fraternity has a 'rule' dating back to its founder, and a special ritual which the members perform when they meet together. This may consist only of the repetition of sacred phrases, or may be more elaborate, as, for instance, the whirlings of the 'dancing dervishes' (the Mevlevi order) or the performances of the Rifai or 'howling dervishes', who, while in a state of ecstasy, eat live coals and glass and cut themselves with knives, as do the Aissawa (Isawiya), a sect widespread in Libya. The practices of the Rifai are of special interest: it was their Sheikh who, at the *doseh* ceremony, rode his horse over the bodies of the prostrate devotees, while the belief of this order in their immunity to snake-poison is implicit; thus not many years ago in Egypt a member who was bitten by a poisonous snake was so convinced of his safety that he refused all treatment, with the result that he died within a few hours.

The Senussi order occupies a unique position among Muslim fraternities, if only on account of the exaggerated importance formerly attributed to it by the French. The order was founded by Sidi Mohammed ben Ali el Senussi, who died in 1859 and was succeeded by his son Sidi el Mahdi. These two men gained many adherents for their order in Cyrenaica, Tripolitania, the Western Desert of Egypt, and in parts of the Sahara and Arabia. The centre of the order was established at Jaghbub in Cyrenaica and afterwards in the distant oasis of Kulfra. The order did much to control the wild Bedouin of the desert, to give them religious instruction, and to represent their interests in matters concerning the Turkish administration. It later led them in their resistance to the French and the Italians, and in an attack on British forces in Egypt during the 1914–18 war. The present head of the order, Sayyid Idris al-Senussi, is also the king of Libya.

Apart from the Hamitic Falasha described in Chapter 5, Jews other than recent immigrants from Europe are confined to North Africa. The Sephardim, the descendants of the Jews expelled from Spain and Portugal at the end of the fifteenth century, generally exhibit the physical characters of their *confrères* still living in this part of Europe. The 'indigenous' Jews of North Africa are for the most part low mesocephals with an average cephalic index (Tunis) of 78.

The Jewesses of Algeria and Tunisia have generally been considered pleasing:

... many can even be called beautiful. Their big black eyes are full of expression, their long black hair and vivacious features give them a charming appearance. But their size is appalling; most of them are rather over than under two hundred pounds, and they have absolutely no shape. But this is in accordance with the Oriental notion of feminine beauty. ...

The long isolated Jews of the Mzab oasis in southern Algeria are described as dolichocephals with a cephalic index (living) of 73. Whether this is accurate or not, there is no doubt that North African Jews are far more dolichocephalic than their Eastern European co-religionists, the percentage (living) being of the following order:

	C.I.	Europe	N. Africa
under 80	. .	25	71
80–85	.	66	28

It may be interesting to add that of Yemenite Jews some 93 per cent. have a cephalic index of under 80.

One other cultural wave has reached Africa. Outrigger canoes, essentially Indonesian, are found on the island of Zanzibar and the neighbouring coast. These must be regarded as an extreme cultural extension westwards of the Indonesian element of Madagascar, though there is no evidence of the admixture of this foreign stock with the natives of Africa, apart perhaps from the population of Lamu.

Appendix 1 Literature

THE MOST SERVICEABLE DESCRIPTIONS of individual groups or tribes are contained in the series of short but comprehensive monographs published by the International African Institute (London) under the general title, *Ethnographic Survey of Africa* (1950– ; in progress). Each monograph has a detailed bibliography and a good map.

The works listed below, for Chapter 1, either deal with Africa generally, or are collections of studies covering various parts of the continent; those for the other chapters include regional surveys and some outstanding accounts of important tribes.

Chapter 1

BAUMANN, H., THURNWALD, R., and WESTERMANN, D. *Völkerkunde von Afrika.* Essen, 1939. (French trans., Paris, 1948.)

BERNATZIK, H. (ed.). *Afrika: Handbuch der angewandten Völkerkunde.* 2 vols. Munich, 1951.

FORDE, D. (ed.). *African Worlds: Studies in the Cosmological Ideas and Social Values of African Peoples.* 1954.

FORTES, M., and EVANS-PRITCHARD, E. E. (eds.). *African Political Systems.* 1940.

GREENBERG, J. 'Studies in African Linguistic Classification', *Southwestern J. Anthrop.*, vols. 5 (1949), 6 (1950).

HADDON, A. C. *The Races of Man and their Distribution.* Cambridge, 1925.

LEROI-GOURHAN, A., and POIRIER, J. *Ethnologie de l'Union Française, I: Afrique.* Paris, 1953.

RADCLIFFE-BROWN, A. R., and FORDE, C. D. (eds.). *African Systems of Kinship and Marriage.* 1950.

WERNER, A. *The Language Families of Africa*. 2nd ed., 1925.

WESTERMANN, D. *The African To-Day and To-Morrow*. 3rd ed., 1929; *Geschichte Afrikas: Staatenbildungen südlich der Sahara*. Cologne, 1952.

Chapter 2

SCHAPERA, I. *The Khoisan Peoples of South Africa: Bushmen and Hottentots*. 1930.

SCHEBESTA, P. *Die Bambuti-Pygmäen vom Ituri*. 3 vols. Brussels, 1938–50; *Les Pygmées du Congo-Belge*. Brussels, 1952.

TREVOR, J. C. 'The Physical Characters of the Sandawe', *J. Roy. Anthrop. Inst.*, vol. 77 (1947).

Chapters 3 and 4

EVANS-PRITCHARD, E. E. *Witchcraft, Oracles and Magic among the Azande*. Oxford, 1937.

FORTES, M. *The Dynamics of Clanship among the Tallensi* (1945); *The Web of Kinship among the Tallensi* (1949).

HERSKOVITS, M. J. *Dahomey*. 2 vols. New York, 1938.

KABERRY, P. *Women of the Grasslands*. 1952. [Bamenda of West Cameroon].

LABOURET, H. *Paysans d'Afrique occidentale*. Paris, 1941.

MEEK, C. K. *Law and Authority in a Nigerian Tribe*. 1937. [Ibo].

NADEL, S. F. *A Black Byzantium* (1942) [Nupe of Nigeria]; *The Nuba* (1946).

RATTRAY, R. S. *Ashanti* (Oxford, 1923); *Religion and Art in Ashanti* (Oxford, 1937); *Ashanti Law and Constitution* (Oxford, 1929).

VEDDER, H. *Die Bergdama*. 2 vols. Hamburg, 1923.

Chapter 5

BATRAWI, A. M. 'The Racial History of Egypt and Nubia', *J. Roy. Anthrop. Inst.*, vols 75 (1945), 76 (1946).

NADEL, S. F. 'Notes on Beni Amer Society', *Sudan Notes and Records*, vol. 26 (1945).

PAUL, A. *A History of the Beja Tribes of the Sudan*. Cambridge, 1954.

SELIGMAN, C. G. 'Some Aspects of the Hamitic Problem in the Anglo-Egyptian Sudan', *J. Roy. Anthrop. Inst.*, vol. 43 (1913).

SERGI, G. *Africa: Antropologia della Stirpa Camitica*. Turin, 1897.

Chapter 6

COON, C. S. 'Tribes of the Rif', *Harvard African Studies*, vol. 9 (1931).

KOLLER, A. *Essai sur l'esprit du Berbère marocain*. Fribourg, 1949.

MAUNIER, R. *Coutumes algériennes.* Paris, 1945.
RODD, F. R. *People of the Veil.* 1926. [Tuareg].
SERGI, G. *The Mediterranean Race.* 1901.

Chapter 7

DRIBERG, J. H. *The Lango.* 1923.
EVANS-PRITCHARD, E. E. *The Nuer* (Oxford, 1940); *Kinship and Marriage among the Nuer* (Oxford, 1951); *Nuer Religion* (Oxford, 1956).
GULLIVER, P. H. *The Family Herds.* 1955. [Jie and Turkana].
HOFMAYR, W. *Die Shilluk.* Vienna, 1925.
MERKER, M. *Die Masai.* Berlin, 1910.
SELIGMAN, C. G. and B. Z. *Pagan Tribes of the Nilotic Sudan.* 1932.

Chapter 8

ASHTON, H. *The Basuto.* 1952.
COLSON, E., and GLUCKMAN, M. (eds.). *Seven Tribes of British Central Africa.* 1951.
DE CLEENE, N. *Inleiding tot de Congoleesche Volkenkunde.* Antwerp, 1943. (French ed., Antwerp, 1944.)
JUNOD, H. A. *The Life of a South African Tribe.* 2nd ed., 2 vols. 1927. [Tsonga].
KRIGE, E. J. and J. D. *The Realm of a Rain-Queen.* 1943. [Lobedu]
KUPER, H. *An African Aristocracy.* 1947. [Swazi]
MAES, J., and BOONE, O. *Les Peuplades du Congo-Belge.* Brussels, 1935.
RICHARDS, A. I. *Land, Labour, and Diet in Northern Rhodesia.* 1939. [Bemba]
SCHAPERA, I. (ed.). *The Bantu-Speaking Tribes of South Africa.* 1937.

Chapter 9

CULWICK, A. T. and G. M. *Ubena of the Rivers.* 1935.
DUNDAS, C. *Kilimanjaro and its People.* 1924. [Chaga]
GROTTANELLI, V. L. *Pescatori dell'Oceano Indiano.* Rome, 1955. [Bajuni]
KENYATTA, J. *Facing Mount Kenya.* 1938. [Kikuyu]
LINDBLOM, G. *The Akamba.* Upsala, 1920.
ROSCOE, J. *The Baganda.* 1911.
WAGNER, G. *The Bantu of North Kavirondo.* 2 vols. 1949, 1956.
WILSON, M. *Good Company.* 1951. [Nyakyusa]

Chapter 10

EVANS-PRITCHARD, E. E. *The Sanusi of Cyrenaica*. Oxford, 1949.

MACMICHAEL, H. A. *A History of the Arabs in the Sudan*. 2 vols. Cambridge, 1922.

MURRAY, G. W. *Sons of Ishmael: a study of the Egyptian Bedouin*. 1935.

MINER, H. *The Primitive City of Timbuctoo*. Princeton, 1953.

SELIGMAN, C. G. and B. Z. 'The Kababish, a Sudan Arab Tribe', *Harvard African Studies, Varia Africana*, vol. 2 (1918).

Appendix 2 Height Conversion Table

CONVERSION table in inches and centimetres of heights between 5 and 6 feet (correct to about a quarter of an inch).

cm.	in.	cm.	in.	cm.	in.	cm.	in.
152	60	160	63	168	66	176	$69\frac{1}{4}$
153	$60\frac{1}{4}$	161	$63\frac{1}{2}$	169	$66\frac{1}{2}$	177	$69\frac{3}{4}$
154	$60\frac{1}{2}$	162	$63\frac{3}{4}$	170	67	178	70
155	61	163	64	171	$67\frac{1}{4}$	179	$70\frac{1}{2}$
156	$61\frac{1}{2}$	164	$64\frac{1}{2}$	172	$67\frac{3}{4}$	180	71
157	$61\frac{3}{4}$	165	65	173	68	181	$71\frac{1}{4}$
158	62	166	$65\frac{1}{4}$	174	$68\frac{1}{2}$	182	$71\frac{1}{2}$
159	$62\frac{1}{2}$	167	$65\frac{3}{4}$	175	69	183	72

Ninety-five per cent. of the measurements which the student will meet fall between these limits; larger or smaller measurements stated in the metric system are easily converted if it be remembered that 1 inch almost equals 2·5 cm. and that 6 inches is approximately 15 cm.

Index

Ababda, 64–66
Abaka, 111
Abarambo, 57
Abukaya, 111
Acholi, 111
Achua, 26
Afar, *see* Danakil
Agau, 74
age grades (sets), 39, 106–7, 142
Agumba, 143
'Ahl Ibl', 152
'Ahl Sawaki', 153
Aikwe, 13
Ajawa, *see* Yao
Akan, 40, 41 et seqq.
Akka, 27
Amarar, 64
Amazons, 45–47
Ambo, 121, 122, 125–6, 130
Amharic language, 74
ancestor worship, 44, 108, 127–30,
  143, 146
Angas, 52
Angica, *see* Teke
Ankole, 101
Anuak, 111
Anziques, *see* Teke
Arabs:
  classification, 152–3
  in Egypt, 154
  in North Africa, 81, 86–87, 150–1

Arabs (*contd.*):
  in West Africa, 155–6
  physical characters, 150–1, 154
  religious confraternities, 156–8
  tribal organization, 153
Artega, 64
Ashanti, 32, 40–45, 54
Ashraf, 64
Aturu, 111
Auen, 13
Aulad Ali, 154
Aushi, 130
Aujila, 83
Azande, 57–58

Baca, 124
Baggara, 152–3, 155, 156
Baghirmi, 38
Bambara, 34, 35 et seqq.
'Bantoid' language, 54
Bantu, 8–10
  cattle, 127
  Central, 120 et seqq.
  classification, 119–23
  definition of term, 117–18
  delimitation, 117 et seqq.
  Eastern, 119, 137 et seqq.
  languages, 5, 54, 99, 117–18
  Southern, 119–30
    ancestor worship, 127–8
    mode of life, 127

Bantu, Southern (*contd.*):
  mutilations, 122–3
  physical characters, 121–2
  social organization, 123–7
  Western, 119, 130–6
  See also under tribal names
Bantu Kavirondo (Luyia), 137
Barabaig, 102
Barabra (Nubi), 61–62, 70 et seqq.
Baraka, doctrine of, 90–92, 114
Barba (Borgu), 37
Barbary pirates, 86
Barea, 56, 72
Bari-speaking tribes, 55, 79, 102, 109–10, 111, 116
Basuto nation, 123, 125
Beir, 111
Beja, 61, 63–71, 73
Belanda, 111
Bemba, 130
Beni Amer, 64–65, 72, 73, 74
Beni Hillal, 151–2
Beni 'Ukba, 154
Benin, 32, 40–41
Berberine, *see* Barabra
Berbers, 81–92, 150
Bergdama (Haukhoin), 59–60
Beriberi, *see* Kanembu
Berta, 55
Bini, 53
Birom, 52
Bisa, 130
Bisharin, 64, 65
Bogos, 72, 73, 74
Bomvu, 124
Bongo, 57
Borana, 76, 77
Bornu, Kingdom of, 38, 39, 52, 155–6
Bororo Fulani, 97–98
Buduma, 39
Buganda, Kingdom of, 137, 139
Bulom, 33, 39
Bunyoro, 137
Burun, 56

Bushmen:
  ancient origin, 8–10
  art, 16, 18
  distribution, 11
  language, 7–8, 12–13
  mutilations, 122–3
  physical characters, 12
  religious beliefs, 15
  social organization and customs, 13–15
Bushongo Empire, 55, 130, 134, 135

calendar customs, Egyptian, 69
cannibalism, 32, 56, 136
Cape Coloured, 17
cattle, 67, 104, 112–13, 127
cephalic index, 3–4
Chaga, 107, 140, 145, 146
Chokwe (Kioko), 130–1
Chopi, 121
Christianity in Ethiopia, 74–76
clan, 2
Copts, 68–69
Cushites, 73
Cushitic languages, 72–73

Dagomba, 37
Dahomey, 33, 37, 40, 45–47
Danagla, 71
Danakil (Afar), 62, 74, 78–79
Dar Fung, 55–56
Darfur, 55, 153
Dargu, 55
Dar Hamid, 153
dead, disposal of:
  Bushmen, 15
  Eastern Bantu,
    Chaga, 146
    Kamba, 143
    Kikuyu, 144–5
    Nyanja, 149
  Hottentots, 24–25
  interlacustrine Bantu, 139–40
  Lotuko, 110

dead (*contd.*):
  Nilo-Hamites, 108
  predynastic Egyptians, 64, 65
  pygmies, 28–29
  Southern Bantu, 128
Dinka, 111, 112–13, 115–16
divine kings, 53–54, 113–16, 134–5
Dorobo (Okiek), 79–80, 102, 143
Dyola (Felup), 39
Dyula, 35

Efé, 28, 29
Efik, 40, 47
Egyptians, 57 et seqq.
  predynastic:
    burial, 64, 65
    in North Africa, 63, 82, 85
    physical characters, 63–64, 65
Erythriotes, 63
Ethiopic languages, 74
'Europeans', 100, 138
Ewe-speaking peoples, 32, 40
exhumation of dead, 110, 146

Falasha, 'black' Jews, 75–76, 158
Fang, *see* Pangwe
Fanti, 40, 43
Fellata, *see* Fulani
Felup, *see* Dyola
fetish, 2
Feyadicha, 71
Fingo, 120, 122
Fiote (Fjort), 133
Fipa, 140
fire, sacred, 38, 59, 60, 128–9, 140
Fjort, *see* Fiote
Fulfulde language, 98–99
Fula, *see* Fulani
Fulani, 37, 39, 49, 50, 51, 96–99, 136
Fulani Emirates, 49–51, 97
Fulbe, 62, 96, *see also* Fulani
Fur, 55

Galikwe, 13
Galla, 62, 74, 76–78, 137, 141, 147
Ganda, 101, 137 et seqq.
Garamantes, ancient, 96
Ge'ez language, 73–74
geographical factors, 8
Giryama, 141, 147
Gogo, 140
Gola, 39
Gonaqua, 17
Griqua, 17
Grunshi, *see* Gurunsi
Guanche, 62, 86
Guinea tribes, 40, 47–48
Gurunsi, 37, 38
Gwari, 52

Habbania, 155
Habe, 50
Hadendoa, 64, 65, 67, 73
half-breeds, 16–17
Hameg, 56
Hamites:
  immigration of, 100–2
  influence in Africa, 8, 31, 62–63
  kinship with Semites, 62–63
  language, 5, 62
  physical characters and types, 61–63, 82–86
Hamiticized Negroes, main divisions, 31, 101
Harabi, 155
Hatsa, 7
Haukhoin, *see* Bergdama
Hausa, 35, 37, 38–39, 49, 50 et seqq.
Hausa states, 51
Hawazma, 155
Haya, 137
Hehe, 140
Heikum, 13
Herero, 60, 121 et seqq.
Hiechware, 13, 14
'High Nilotic' group, 56

Hottentots,
  avoidance between relatives, 20–21
  burial, 24–25
  comparison with Bushmen, 18
  half-breeds, 16–17
  language, 7–8
  mutilations, 19
  mythology and religious beliefs, 21–25
  origin and distribution, 16–17
  physical characters, 16
  social organization, 17–18, 18–21
Howeitat, 155
Hukwe, 13
Huma, 101–2, 137, 138–9
human sacrifice, 32, 40, 45–46, 138, 139–40
Humr, 155
Hurutshe, 121

Ibibio, 33, 40
Ibo, 40
Ijaw, 47
Ila, 130
Indonesian elements, 159
initiation, see puberty ceremonies
Iru, 101, 138, 139
Ituri forest-dwellers, 29

Jaga, 131
Jallonke, 35
Jaluo, 111
Jar, 52
Jews, 158–9, see also Falasha
Jolof, see Wolof
Jukun, 52. 53–54
Jur, 57

Kababish, 153, 154
Kabyles, 83–84, 87–90
Kafficho, 72, 73
'Kaffirs', 121
Kalanga, 120

Kaliko, 57
Kamba, 107, 140, 142–5
Kanem, 38
Kanembu, 38–39
Kanuri, 38, 39, 156
Karamojong, 102
Karanga, 120
Kasongo, Kingdom of, 132
Kassena, 38
Kassonke, 35
Kavirondo, 110–11
Kawahla, 153
Kazembe, Kingdom of, 132
Kenana, 153
Kenuz, 71
Keyo (Elgeyo), 102
Kgatla, 121, 123
Kharga, 83
Khoisan, 5
Kikuyu, 102, 107, 140, 143, 143–5
Kioko, see Chokwe
Kipsigis (Lumbwa), 102, 104, 108
Kissi, 39
Kituara Empire, 137 et seqq.
Kololo, 124
Konde, 140
Kongo, Kingdom of, 130, 131–2, 133
Kongo, 133
Korana, 17
Korekore, 120
Kpelle, 39
Kru, 39–40
Kuba, 132
Kunum, 56
Kwa language, 32, 40
Kwanyama, 125
Kwena, 121, 123, 125

Lango, 110, 111
Lendu, 57, 111
Libyans, 62, 63
Lotuko, 102, 109–10, 111, 116
Lozi, 130
Luba, 111, 132, 133

Luba-Bemba, 130
Luba-Hemba, 130
Luba-Lunda group, 130
Luluwa, 130
Lumbwa, 102
Lunda, 130, 131
Lunda Empire, 131–2
Luo, 110, 111

Ma'aza, 154
Madi, 111, 112
Magiabra, 83
Mahas, 71
Mahdiya, 156
Mai Munene, Kingdom of, 132
Makaraka, 58
Makua, 140, 141
Malinke, 34
Mamprussi, 37
Mamvu, 57
Mandara, 39
Mande, 35
Mandingo tribes, 34, 35, 53
Mangbetu, 57
Manyika, 120
Masai, 67, 79, 102–8, 140, 143,
    144, 145, 146
Mbala (Bushongo), 132, 134
Melle, 35
Mende, 33, 39
Messiria, 155
Midgan, 79
milk, sanctity of, 23, 67, 105
Mittu, 111
Mongo group, 130, 132, 133
Moru, 111
Mosgu, 39
Mossi, 37 et seqq.
Mpondo, 120, 126
Muhammadan Kingdoms, 38–39,
    49

Naman, 17 et seqq.
Nandi, 67, 79, 80, 102–8

Nankani, 38
Naron, 13, 14
nasal index, 4
!nau, 21–25
Ndau, 120
Ndebele (Tebele), 120, 124
Ndogo, 57
Ndonga, 125
Ndwandwe, 124
Negrillo (pygmy):
    classical references to, 26
    distribution, 26
    language, 8, 29
    physical characters, 27
    relation to other races, 11, 29
    religion, 28
Negro:
    distribution, 30–32
    early references to, 30
    Hamitic influence, 8, 31, 100 et
        seqq.
    languages, 7
    physical and cultural characters,
        32 et seqq.
Negroids, 84
Ngala, 133
Ngendi, 134
Ngonde, 140
Ngongo, 134
Ngoni, 124, 141
Nguni, 120
Ngwaketse, 121, 125
Ngwane, 124
Ngwato, 121, 125
Nilo-Hamites:
    age grades, 106–7
    burial customs, 108
    cattle, 8
    definition, 101–2
    language, 102
    medicine men, 107
    religion, 107–8
    tribes, 102–4
Nilotes:
    classification, 110–12

Nilotes (*contd.*):
  comparison with other groups,
    56–57, 111–12
  language, 111
  physical and psychical
    characters, 112 et seqq.
Nilotic, 110 et seqq.
Nordic type, 84–87
Nuba, 54–56
Nubi, *see* Barabra
Nuer, 111–13
Nupe, 40, 52
Nurab, 64
Nyakyusa, 140
Nyamwezi, 137
Nyanja, 141, 147–9
Nyankole, 138–40
Nyika, 140–1
Nyoro, 138–40

Okiek (Dorobo), 79
Old Cape Hottentots, 17
Oromo, 76–78
Oshyeba, 135–6
outcast tribes, 79–80
outrigger canoes, 159

Pangwe (Fang), 131, 135–6
Pedi, 121, 123
Peuls, *see* Fulani
physical characters, terminology
  and definitions, 2–5
Pokomo, 140
Pokot, *see* Suk
Portuguese, 147
primary races of Africa, 5
puberty ceremonies, 14, 23–24,
  53, 122–3, 145–6
pygmies, *see* Negrillos

Queen of Sheba, 75

race, definition and criteria of, 2–5
rain-making and rain-makers, 15,
  107, 109–10, 113, 115–16

Rasheida (Zebediye), 156
Rehoboth, 17
religion, 2
religious confraternities, 156–8
Riffian tribes, 84–85
rites de passage, 21 et seqq.
Rizeigat, 155
Rolong, 121
Ronga, 120
Rundi, 137
Rwanda, 137

Sāb, 79
Sagara, 140
Saho, 74
Sambara, 140
Sandawe, 16
Sango, 140
secret societies, 33–34, 39–40
semi-Bantu, 135–6
Semites:
  cultural influence, 61, 74
  languages, 5–7, 73–74
  recent entry into Africa, 8
  see also Arabs
Senussi, 157–8
Serer, 34–35
Shangana, 121
Shankalla tribes, 56
Shawia, 82–83, 84
Shila, 130
Shilluk, 39, 44, 107, 111–15, 135
Shir, 116
Shona, 120, 121, 123, 125
Shuwa, 156
Siwa, 83
snake cult, 51, 55, 77, 144
Soko, 133
Somali, 61, 74, 78, 147
Songe, 130, 132
Songhai, Kingdom of, 35, 37, 38
Songo-Meno group, 130
Soninke, 35
stature, table of measurements, 3,
  see also Appendix II

Strandlopers, 11
Sudanic languages, 7, 31–32, 70, 99, 111
Suk (Pokot), 102, 104, 105–6, 108
Sukuma, 137
Swahili, 140, 141, 146–7
Swazi, 120, 122, 125

Ta'aisha, 155
Tallensi, 38
Taita, 107, 140, 145
Tannekwe, 13
Tawana, 121–5
Teke (Angica, Anziques), 131
Tem, 37
Temne, 33, 39
Teso, 102
Tetela, 132, 133–4
Tetwa, 124
Thembu, 120
Tibu, 39, 62, 96
Tigrinya language, 64, 74
Tiv, 52–53
Tlhaping, 121
To Bedawi language, 64
Tomal, 79
Toposa, 102
totem, 2
trade routes, 50
'Transvaal Ndebele', 120
Tsonga, 120, 122 et seqq.

Tswa, 120
Tswana, 121 et seqq.
Tuareg, 37, 62, 92–96
Tukolor, 34, 35
Tungur, 55
Turkana, 102, 104
Twi-speaking peoples, 7, 32

Vei, 35
Venda, 120, 121

Walamo, 73
Warjawa, 52
Wata, 72, 80
water, sanctity of, 23–24
Wira, 111
Wolof (Jolof), 34–35
Wongo-Lele-Bushongo congeries, 130

Xhosa, 120, 122, 123

Yaka, 131
Yao (Ajawa), 141, 147–8
Yibir, 79
Yoruba-speaking peoples, 7, 33, 40, 41, 47–48, 53

Zebediye, see Rasheida
Zezuru, 120
Zulu, 101, 118, 120, 122 et seqq.

DATE DUE